YORK NOTES

The Duchess of Malfi

John Webster

Note by Stephen Sims

 Longman    York Press

Stephen Sims is hereby identified as author of this work in accordance with Section 77 of the Copyright, Designs and Patents Act 1988

YORK PRESS
322 Old Brompton Road, London SW5 9JH

PEARSON EDUCATION LIMITED
Edinburgh Gate, Harlow,
Essex CM20 2JE, United Kingdom
Associated companies, branches and representatives throughout the world

First published 2000

ISBN 0–582–32912–4

Designed by Vicki Pacey
Phototypeset by Gem Graphics, Trenance, Mawgan Porth, Cornwall
Colour reproduction and film output by Spectrum Colour
Produced by Addison Wesley Longman China Limited, Hong Kong

CONTENTS

AUTHOR OF THIS NOTE & ACKNOWLEDGEMENTS

Stephen Sims read English at Exeter and was a Senior Lecturer at the University of Birmingham. He is a freelance teacher and writer.

In a sense this Note is multi-authored and due acknowledgement of that is made here to those others: Annalisa, Fran and Hugh for help in attaining a modest level of word-processing skills; Eva Cruz of Queen Mary and Westfield College, University of London and the Universities of Salamanca and Alcala de Henares, together with Melville Hope of Queen Elizabeth College, Crediton, and Karen Edwards, Renaissance scholar and friend, for critical ideas and constructive correction; Michael Nath of the University of Exeter, as dedicated to his students as he is to learning and I am to him, without whom this Note would not have been written; and Sue, my partner, who bore up well as yet another book entailed neglect and a falling off in the walking of the cats.

PART ONE

INTRODUCTION

HOW TO STUDY A PLAY

Studying on your own requires self-discipline and a carefully thought-out work plan in order to be effective.

- Drama is a special kind of writing (the technical term is 'genre') because it needs a performance in the theatre to arrive at a full interpretation of its meaning. Try to imagine that you are a member of the audience when reading the play. Think about how it could be presented on the stage, not just about the words on the page.

- Drama is always about conflict of some sort (which may be below the surface). Identify the conflicts in the play and you will be close to identifying the large ideas or themes which bind all the parts together.

- Make careful notes on themes, character, plot and any sub-plots of the play.

- Why do you like or dislike the characters in the play? How do your feelings towards them develop and change?

- Playwrights find non-realistic ways of allowing an audience to see into the minds and motives of their characters, for example soliloquy, aside or music. Consider how such dramatic devices are used in *The Duchess of Malfi*.

- Think of the playwright writing the play. Why were these particular arrangements of events, characters and speeches chosen?

- Cite exact sources for all quotations, whether from the text itself or from critical commentaries. Wherever possible find your own examples from the play to back up your opinions.

- Always express your ideas in your own words.

This York Note offers an introduction to *The Duchess of Malfi* and cannot substitute for close reading of the text and the study of secondary sources.

This is the story of an upper-class dysfunctional family who hate themselves so much that they resort to torture, murder and a predatory contemplation of incest. It is the story of a self-made and clever civil servant who realises, too late, that cunning is no substitute for care. It is the story of a prince who is a young woman, lusty but unfortunately a widow, who makes the grave social mistake of putting passion before position and marries her cultured but too-cautious steward; who is himself not astute enough to know that there is always a glass ceiling to upward mobility. Finally, it is a story of power and corruption in the high places of State and Church, as well as the insidious degradation brought upon the lowly; and of how moral values may have very little to do with the accepted rules. In short, it is a play very much up-to-date for the start of the twenty-first century.

Throughout, the Duchess remains an enigma. We never know her name, though we get to know a great deal about her character. We are bound to warm to someone who is so inclined to let heart rule head. She cares little for the straightjacket that social convention demands of her widowhood and in which her pompous brothers are determined to keep her locked. She chooses to marry a man who seems increasingly unworthy of her as the play proceeds. We marvel at the lack of judgement both of them display in surrounding themselves with inadequate support; a treacherous steward, an unreliable friend, a histrionic maid. We watch her with fascination, as a rabbit does a snake, as she watches her unlovely brothers, one too cold and the other too hot. We are mesmerised by Bosola, the servant with a foot in both camps. And we come to realise, as the Duchess races inevitably towards an horrific but dignified exit, that what destroys her and Bosola is the same characteristic that makes them so vibrant in the play and so compelling to follow – uncompromising energy.

There are some potent themes to look out for which recur throughout the play: secret marriage, inheritance, politics, widowhood, revenge and corruption, the confinements of prison, madness and false religion, good advice and flattery.

T.S. Eliot wrote a poem, 'Whispers of Immortality', whose first two stanzas run:

> Webster was much possessed by death
> And saw the skull beneath the skin;
> And breastless creatures under ground
> Leaned backward with a lipless grin.
>
> Daffodil bulbs instead of balls
> Stared from the sockets of the eyes!
> He knew that thought clings round dead limbs
> Tightening its lusts and luxuries.

Nowadays, Webster is considered to be one of England's most accomplished **Renaissance** playwrights. What happens, however, in people's minds and hearts, shown to us by what they say and what others say about them, is awesome in its contemporary appositeness. Some of the characters watch and plot and hate. Others let go and love. Some are strong and some are weak, some present a devilish cheek and some are just plain wrong.

We witness bad people serve bad people faithfully (Bosola and the Aragon brothers). We see good people let down by good people, who in their turn are let down by other good people (The Duchess, Antonio and Delio).

As audience we are not spared terror and horror and exhaustion.

PART TWO

SUMMARIES & COMMENTARIES

NOTE ON THE TEXT AND ITS SOURCES

As was common practice in his day, Webster's plots were not usually original but 'borrowed' from classical myth, historical narratives or other dramatists. The source for this play lies in a factual story related through a number of different-authored reports, gaining detail and embellishment as it was successively retold. Briefly, the story is first recounted in a novella by Matteo Bandello, a probable witness to some aspects of the drama, and who some critics believe is represented in the play as Delio.

The adaptation in William Painter's *Second Tome of the Palace of Pleasure* (1567) is probably Webster's main source, although he is thought to have used material from other contemporary writers not associated with Bandello's version of the story to embellish his dramatic tale.

Webster employed his own genius to fabricate several departures of the plot he inherited to simplify and intensify theatrical satisfaction for his audience. Chief among these are the amalgamation of the various forces placed in opposition to the Duchess by her brothers into the **persona** of Bosola (literally translated 'bloudy beast'), and the active presence throughout the play of the brothers themselves. Additional subplots are Webster's clever introduction of the Cardinal's mistress Julia, the dumb-show in Loretto, the tortures brought upon his sister by Ferdinand and his ultimate **solipsistic** madness.

We are more fortunate with Webster's masterpiece than with many contemporary texts in that a substantially reliable quarto was available to Okes in 1623 which required very few and minor emendations to the proofs before printing. Evidence of Webster's care and presence in the print room is afforded by certain stage directions being squeezed in between lines or relegated to the margins.

Three further quartos were produced over the next century, none on a par with the quality of the first. One of the merits of the second and subsequent quartos was that certain of the obvious typographical errors that had slipped in were eliminated. In doing so, however, certain other and further errors were introduced. The final quarto, produced in 1708, deliberately shortened the play by intended cuts. In the first prints of the play in 1623 there are four introductory sections; a title page containing an obscure Latin exhortation translated 'If you are not aware of a better play, hear mine', a list of The Actors' Names including the part of Forobosco, a Dedication to the playwright's patron and Commendations by three of his contemporaries, and a Dramatis Personae which curiously includes parts additional to those in The Actors' Names.

This Note refers to the New Mermaids (third) edition of the play, edited by Elizabeth M. Brennan and published by A & C Black, 1993. Although it is based on the first quarto, the editor has standardised where inconsistencies arise, for instance in the varied punctuation and archaic spelling where this would be misleading.

SYNOPSIS

Antonio, chief steward to the young and widowed Duchess of Malfi, has recently returned from the French court, on which he comments favourably to his friend Delio. Their conversation is interrupted by an ex-galley-slave, Bosola, who complains to the Cardinal that he is still unrewarded for past and sinister services.

Whilst Delio and Antonio provide the audience with commentary, Duke Ferdinand, brother to the Duchess and the Cardinal, positions himself centre-stage. Having induced his sister to employ Bosola as head of her stables, he persuades the '**malcontent**' to act as 'intelligencer' and spy on the Duchess's private life. The maid is a silent spectator of the Duchess's brothers' attempt to dissuade their sister from remarrying. Cariola is then an invisible listener to her mistress's wooing of Antonio. That accomplished she is a visible and audible witness at their wedding.

Bosola's disdain of courtly decay is displaced by his angry rejection of Antonio's accusation of ambition. The heavily pregnant Duchess and her retinue enter and Bosola offers her a gift of early-season apricots, which she greedily accepts. The fruit brings on a sudden illness which Antonio believes may be the onset of labour, and thereby fears that their secret will be exposed.

Bosola's spying activities are frustrated by being confined to quarters, along with the rest of the Duchess's staff, a scheme involving trumped up charges of theft that Antonio has devised to prevent anyone finding out about the birth of his son.

Both Antonio and Bosola are on personal and clandestine spying missions and meet by chance at night. Their mutual hostility erupts. Antonio accidentally and unknowingly drops the new baby's horoscope as he leaves and Bosola picks it up, wasting no time in communicating the information it contains back to Rome.

The Cardinal is in Rome with his mistress Julia. Her pillow-talk is as witty as his is cold. Delio, newly arrived, tries with money in the absence of wit to regain the favours of Julia, his former lover. She hears that her husband, old Castruchio, has also recently come from Malfi, and suggests they ask his permission.

The Duke and the Cardinal discuss their sister in Malfi. In anguish Ferdinand grows increasingly intemperate in his accusations of her. The Cardinal loses patience with his brother's extreme views, and prepares to leave the stage. Ferdinand calms, determining to assume an attitude of 'sleep' until he has gained a knowledge of the facts.

After a lapse of time, during which two more children are born to the Duchess, Delio is again in Amalfi where he and his friend Antonio bring each other up to date. Ferdinand also is paying a visit to the Duchess which is causing unease, not least because of his uncharacteristic peaceableness. He equably accepts his sister's rejection of his choice of a suitor for her, and calmly discounts her expressions of anxiety about the court rumours circulating about her. Alone with Bosola, the Duke asks for the key to her bedchamber, explaining he is now going to extract a confession from her.

In the Duchess's room the night begins with happy intimacy. Antonio insists that despite (or even because of) the danger proximity to Ferdinand poses they will pass the night together. Antonio involves Cariola in a juvenile game of hide-and-seek during which Ferdinand enters his sister's room unannounced. She inadvertently betrays herself and he threatens her with death. The Duke departs to Rome in a fury. To divert immediate danger the Duchess constructs a ploy to mock-accuse Antonio of false stewardship. His banishment in the face of her public discrediting allows him to make a peremptory escape with their oldest son to Ancona where he expects her soon to join him. Alone, she finds Bosola sympathetic to Antonio and, in a moment of unguardedness, confides in him that Antonio is her husband and the father of their three children. She then trusts Bosola in the conveying of all her wealth to Antonio. Bosola knows that his despised task of simultaneously serving opposing masters is nearly over.

In Rome the court is rife with speculation as the Cardinal responds to the Emperor's call to arms, and Ferdinand and then Bosola arrive to confer over developments in Malfi. They plan the Duchess's banishment from Ancona.

In the shrine at Loretto, two pilgrims observe the Cardinal's transformation from priest to soldier. In dumb-show with pilgrim commentary, the Duchess and her family are expelled from Ancona. Questions are reasonably asked about the whole legality of these proceedings.

Fleeing from Ancona, the Duchess and her party are overtaken by Bosola who carries a message from Ferdinand asking her to send Antonio to report to the Duke on a matter of business. She declines. Bosola departs empty-handed and the Duchess quickly splits up her group by sending Antonio and their son on to Milan. Their parting is sad though restrained and is no sooner accomplished than Bosola reappears but this time disguised, to take her into 'protection' and escort her back to house-arrest in Malfi. She submits, realising her time of liberty may be over, yet still harbouring hopes for a more settled and optimistic future.

Ferdinand is frustrated that the Duchess is bearing her imprisonment with fortitude. He endeavours to unsettle her composure, under pretence of reconciliation, by meeting her in a darkened room and presenting her with a dead man's hand. Bosola is directed by the Duke to reveal to her a tableau of figures of her husband and son. She assumes their death, not realising that the images are artificial. By now Ferdinand seems to be achieving his intention to cause her to despair. She wishes to die, but her brother only has plans to heighten her mental torture.

The Duchess, although now in a fatalistic calm, still retains her good humour. She hears a disturbance from the neighbouring madhouse and her apartments are then invaded by these residents from next door.

They fail to shake her composure, though they destroy the serenity of her maid. Bosola enters as a herald of death, disguised as 'tomb maker', ushering in executioners, who strangle the Duchess. The dignity of her passing starkly contrasts with the violence accompanying the demise of her unready maid. Ferdinand appears, unmoved by the bodies of the throttled children but profoundly upset by the sight of his inert sister. Cunningly, he blames Bosola for not protecting the Duchess during his (the Duke's) fit of mad jealousy. Bosola, understandably, is appalled at the duplicity of a master who now doubles the insult by offering him, as ghoulish reward, immunity from prosecution for murder. The Duchess revives briefly from her fatal swoon, to hear Bosola's fabrication of Antonio's restoration to amity with her brothers. She finally expires. Bosola's hopes of a better life die with her. He bitterly resolves to proceed to Milan, there to enact his revenge as speedily as possible.

In Milan, Antonio is becoming aware that it may be more difficult to reinstate himself with the Aragon brothers than at first he thought. His lands have been seized by them and then passed on to nonentities. He decides, with Delio's support, to make one last effort at reconciliation with the Cardinal.

The courtiers gather to soothe Ferdinand who has been stricken with lycanthropia and suffers another attack which his physician is unable to control. The stage clears to leave the Cardinal and Bosola in discussion. Julia enters with a call to supper, commenting in an **aside** to the audience how she fancies Bosola. Alone together again, Bosola and the Cardinal plot to kill Antonio. Julia reappears. Finding Bosola alone, she propositions him with determined wooing. He tests her commitment with a task; to discover why the Cardinal is so distracted. After hiding Bosola behind a curtain, she carries out her assignment at the first opportunity. After at first resisting her probing the Cardinal relents, but not without dire warning that the knowledge he is about to impart carries capital danger. He divulges that it was he who was behind the murder of the Duchess. Julia responds by telling him that she cannot keep his secret, (though she does not tell him why – that it is because Bosola has heard their conversation, hiding behind the curtain). The Cardinal makes Julia swear to secrecy, insisting she kiss 'religiously' a Bible whose cover is smeared with poison, thereby enforcing her silence. Bosola emerges from cover and he and the Cardinal continue planning Antonio's demise.

Alone again, Bosola **soliloquises** to the audience that he plans to seek out Antonio and save him from 'these most cruel biters'.

Antonio and Delio are walking near the Cardinal's lodgings. Antonio hears an echo of their conversation which sounds like his wife's ghostly voice. He resolves to seal his fate once and for all, for good or ill, by seeking out her brothers.

Meanwhile, late at night, the Cardinal ensures that he and Bosola will not be disturbed removing and concealing Julia's body. By a combination of threats and promises to his courtiers he gets them to agree an oath as well. They are to ignore any noise from his quarters, however threatening. It is the Cardinal's turn to soliloquise to the audience: as soon as Bosola has served his term, he will die. But Bosola overhears and recognises his danger of knowing too much. In the confusion of darkness he stabs Antonio to death by mistake instead of the Cardinal. He has the servant carry Antonio's body towards the Cardinal's chamber.

Bosola arrives at the Cardinal's lodgings, along with the servant who bears the dead Antonio. Bosola crudely proclaims the Cardinal's death as imminent. The Cardinal cries vainly to his courtiers for help; they anticipate this is a trick to test their loyalty and ignore him as they vowed. Bosola kills the servant to ensure the Cardinal's door remains locked then wounds the Cardinal, but is himself caught off guard by the appearance of Ferdinand. The deluded Duke stabs his brother and, for good measure Bosola, who himself then kills the Duke, and this is soon followed by the Cardinal's death as the courtiers burst in. Bosola, after acquainting them with brief details of the drama to date, himself expires. Delio enters leading in Antonio's son, whom he proclaims as heir.

Detailed summaries

ACT I

SCENE 1   Antonio and Delio's conversation is interrupted by a less harmonious discussion between Bosola and the Cardinal in which demands are unsuccessfully made for reward due for sinister past services

Act I and the first half of Act II are set in Malfi at the Duchess's palace. Delio welcomes back his old friend Antonio after a long absence. The Cardinal enters on the heels of Bosola who seems prepared to serve any ends by any means if the reward is right; which, Antonio observes, is in marked contrast to the good order to be found at the French court.

Bosola and the Cardinal fall into a bitter dialogue. Bosola's demeanour makes no pretence at graciousness. Throughout the scene he chides in a common **prose** whereas the rest of the cast orate in **iambic pentametered blank verse**. The Cardinal rapidly retreats. Antonio and Delio engage in discussion with Bosola, who surlily describes the parasitic nature of court and ecclesia, after which he leaves.

Once more, Antonio is alone with Delio, who explains how Bosola has served sentence in the galleys for a suspected murder carried out on the Cardinal's orders, later released after an act of bravery. This impresses Antonio who regrets the **malcontent**'s bitterness, however, as a threat to the positive features of his nature.

> Right away, Webster identifies a major preoccupation of the play, words; their power to ennoble and debase. Drama and action are rooted in language and speech, and the playwright's **irony** is that it is by language that this authority is bestowed. Antonio contrasts 'noble duty' with pandering. Good counsel will transport the counsellor across those barriers which customarily debar betterment into intimacy.

> Introduced is another preoccupation of the play; vivid **imagery**, contrasting good government with bad, the French court being upheld 'like a common fountain', a contrast with Malfi where some 'poison't near the head, / Death and diseases through the whole land spread' (lines 14–15).

Bosola, like Antonio, eschews flattery and we laud him for that, seeing how uncomfortable he makes the Cardinal by his straight speaking. But this curious kind of truth is unpalatable because it is delivered from a heart of hate to a heart of hate. Note the **tone** of language he flings at the back of his employer/adversary who ignominiously scuttles off, 'haunt' (line 29), 'Slighted' (line 38) and 'this great fellow were able to possess the greatest / devil, and make him worse' (lines 46–7). With careless venom he dismisses both brothers with another **simile**, 'like plum trees, that grow / crooked over standing pools' (lines 49–50), as colourful a description of ripe corruption as it is possible to conceive! And yet because, as Bosola describes it, this is a miserable age when there is no more reward for doing well than doing well, he will still demean himself and 'hang on their ears like a horse-leech, till I were full' (line 53).

Already there is a powerful hint that rather than a court purged will be the concomitance of evil. A good counsellor can only rise to fall. A sad mercenary of a **malcontent** will only see corruption and the disability of disease, 'places in the court are but like beds in the / hospital, where this man's head lies at that man's foot, and / so lower and lower' (lines 66–8).

In Bosola we are introduced to the epitome of anarchy: authority has always had most to fear from those who not only have nothing to gain from it, but also nothing to lose from it. Life without means comes to mean nothing.

[There is no glossary entry where a New Mermaid footnote is available]

23 **court-gall** blister or sore (gall may be a **pun** for gull, a fool)

25 **rails** mocks

71 **suborn'd** induced, caused to be undertaken

SCENE 2   While Delio and Antonio continue as commentators
Ferdinand asserts himself at centre stage. Having
persuaded his sister to employ Bosola, he commissions
Bosola spy on her. Cariola is silent witness to Ferdinand
and the Cardinal's attempts to dissuade the Duchess from
remarrying and invisible witness to the Duchess's
successful attempt to woo Antonio. She becomes a visible
and an audible witness at their wedding

Antonio and Delio are still in discussion. Duke Ferdinand and some of
his courtiers enter. Ferdinand acknowledges Antonio's prowess at
horsemanship but is impatient for action of a more bellicose nature. His
courtiers try to dissuade him, 'It is fitting a soldier arise to be a prince,
but / not necessary a prince descend to be a captain!' (lines 14–15).

Ferdinand indulges in unsporting mockery of one of the older
courtiers in his group; Castruchio is the husband of Julia, who is the
Cardinal's mistress. Conversation descends into trivial bawdiness, the
merits of Ferdinand's horse, its fiery nature, 'begot / by the wind' (lines
38–9). The Duke's flatterers forget themselves to become bold and
make lewd jokes. It is clear they have overstepped their mark. Ferdinand's
reminder is a chilling warning to them that they as 'courtiers should
be my touchwood, take fire when I give / fire; that is, laugh when I laugh'
(lines 44–5). Ferdinand then compliments Antonio on his riding skills.
Wisely but resolute, he does not attempt to return the flattery.

The Duchess enters with her maid Cariola, her Cardinal brother
and his mistress Julia. Antonio indulges in a further **ironic aside**
concerning the Cardinal's temperament; that he is, despite an extrovert
appearance, gloomy and devious, 'Some good he hath done' (line 89). He
adds that Ferdinand is just as perverse, a theme echoing Bosola's earlier
assessment of the Cardinal, 'this great fellow were able to possess the
greatest / devil, and make him worse' (I.1.46–7).

By contrast, Antonio discusses the Duchess in such glowing terms
that Delio accuses him of exaggeration. Antonio will soon have an
opportunity of putting his opinion to the test. Cariola summons him to
attend the Duchess in half an hour.

The scene shifts to Ferdinand who persuades the Duchess to take
Bosola into her service, after which the stage clears again so that only the

princely brothers remain. They conspire who shall spy upon their sister for them. Bosola enters and once again, the Cardinal leaves hastily. Ferdinand defers to his older brother's choice of intelligencer and lays a bribe upon the table. Bosola seems ready enough to cut a throat but is unhappy with what is now proposed. Ferdinand explains his motives, 'she's a young widow; / I would not have her marry again' (lines 176–7). Bosola tries to reject the bribe, declaring Ferdinand 'a corrupter, me an impudent traitor' (line 186), but recognises that this secret assignation goes with the position secured for him as master of the Duchess's horse; 'my corruption / Grew out of horse dung. I am your creature' (lines 207–8).

Ferdinand, backed by the Cardinal, endeavours to persuade their sister, widowed but young, not to remarry. The Cardinal offers insight from his own litany of hypocrisy in sexual **innuendo** and **dramatic irony**, 'The marriage night / Is the entrance into some prison' (lines 243–4); no doubt the reason why he enjoys Julia as mistress rather than as a wife. The brothers believe they have been successful when they hear the Duchess say 'I'll never marry –' (line 223), disregarding the fact that they have interrupted her sentence in mid-flow. They leave her with Cariola to whom she confesses 'Let old wives report / I winked, and chose a husband' (lines 267–8).

The maid hides and Antonio reports to the Duchess who asks him to write her will. Duchess and steward discuss the benefits of marriage, a course of action he counsels. She observes his bloodshot eye and, as remedy, offers him 'my wedding ring, / And I did vow never to part with it, / But to my second husband' (lines 324–6). Suddenly their discourse has become intimate as he discerns her intentions. He fears his admiration for her as mad ambition.

The Duchess is frustrated by her steward's cautious awareness of their different status. She chances a bold declaration, 'The misery of us, that are born great, / We are forc'd to woo, because none dare woo us' (lines 357–8). Antonio thinks of her brothers' reaction. She reacts by challenging the power of **tragedy**; 'All discord ... / Is only to be pitied, and not fear'd' (lines 384–5). Cariola bursts in to the declaration of a marriage contract, as adequate in their eyes as anything the church can offer them. Antonio leads the Duchess off to their marriage bed and Cariola anticipates confrontation to come; enumerating again the two facets of **tragedy**, fear and pity, 'it shows / A fearful madness: I owe her much of pity' (lines 418–9).

Throughout this long scene the audience is introduced to the rest of the major themes; at its end is the climax which will direct the destiny of the rest of the play. By then Antonio will have come out of the shadowy world of commentator, through the spotlight of counsellor and into the secret role of husband.

The play has much to say about counsel. A widow who is also a prince cannot survive in a male world without sound advice and the Duchess's brothers are only too aware of this. They skew their injunction to their own purposes, which for her means perpetual widowhood. But this single parent already has two children and she is still young (most estimates age her about eighteen) and vivacious.

A traditional destination for widows is the convent. But young widows are not a peaceful influence in the virginal atmosphere of convent life. And this attractive widow has a personal inclination to remarry.

A symbol throughout the scene is the ring. Ferdinand wants to know the identity of the successful lancer who has removed the suspended rope ring. A number of critics suggest that this 'ring oft'nest' (line 6) is a sexually suggestive **pun**. The **irony** is that it is this same Antonio who receives the Duchess's ring in a playful scene of seduction. The jewel Ferdinand bestows on Antonio now is reminiscent of the jewel of Malfi, the Duchess, to be bestowed on him at their secret marriage.

But the ring has a more sinister connotation; the Duchess, two of her children and her serving woman will be murdered in Act IV and the manner of their deaths will be by being strangled with a ring of rope.

Antonio's feat of horsemanship introduces strong animal **imagery** and stirs Ferdinand's ambition for warlike activity. His courtiers try to dissuade him but he sees battle as a test of virility and so is well pleased with their opinion of his Spanish steed. His banter at a prowess of fecundity is **ironic** in the face of his own inhibitiveness. All this is in stark contrast to an imminent conversation he has with Bosola who, in his reluctant agreement to work secretly for him as well as openly for her, likens his 'bribe of shame' (line 211) to 'my corruption / Grew out of horse dung'. Bosola admits he is 'your creature' (line 208), a loyal replica of those corrupt princes he serves, ready to do their foul bidding for reward, 'a very quaint invisible devil in flesh' (line 181).

Ferdinand reminds him that although he may find his job as intelligencer in the Duchess's household unsavoury, his life and livelihood depend upon this his creator. Bosola is cast as the ultimate servant; he would prefer to cut throats. He used to be a galley-slave. Now this **malcontent** must turn his hand to being a spy.

Bosola fulfils the role of malcontent to which later will be added that of melancholic. His disaffection is revealed in mutinous speech. He speaks his mind whatever the consequences. That evokes contrasting responses in us; we like his honesty but know he will not be reined in by any considerations of sensitivity.

Melancholy is usually a mellow attribute. Antonio uses this adjective to describe the Cardinal's 'inward character' (line 80); outwardly extrovert, agile and accomplished, inwardly jealous and devious. His cunning demands the employment of 'political monsters' … 'flatterers, panders, intelligencers, atheists' (lines 84–5). He bribes his way through the world under the guise of the church. Antonio, hardly of scintillating wit, bestows on the Cardinal a supreme **irony**, 'Some good he hath done' (line 89). Ferdinand is sinister too, but mercurial and inconsistent, 'like a foul black cobweb to a spider' (line 100).

Antonio concludes his character sketches of the main **protagonists** with the Duchess. But for her he uses noble epithets. She is able to make even the sick dance. She is a model for all. Even the lascivious have their vain hopes quelled. (Is this self-rebuke reflected in his muted response to her later wooing?) The **imagery** used to describe her has more of heaven than earth about it.

He is in for a rude awakening. She brings herself down to his level in her wooing; and when achieved, she leads him with great alacrity 'by the hand / Unto your marriage bed' (lines 409–10). Her ardent earthiness risks a risqué **metaphor** about a tantalising ploy, to 'Lay a naked sword between us, keep us chaste' (line 414). It is certainly a more cheerful weapon than the one Ferdinand has pointed at her earlier. Some critics have identified in the Duke's **imagery** a phallic reference, a first inkling of her brother's incestuous feelings towards her. There can be little doubt as to her **innuendo** to Antonio.

The Cardinal and the Duke 'would not have her marry again' (line 176), to marry twice is 'most luxurious' (line 218). They warn her against corruption, lustful pleasures, hypocrisy and flattery, all to be major themes in a play in which they will be chief culprits. They threaten that marriage is a prison; the **irony** being that she will end up in a prison of their making, 'free' of her marriage.

But in wit she is a match for their threats. She employs the jewel **metaphor**, and gives it a twist. Diamonds 'are of most value / … pass't through most jewellers hands' (lines 220–1). To all their advice she wittily rejoins an **oxymoron** 'This is terrible good counsel' (line 232). Their counsel, of course, is in direct contradiction to Antonio's, whose word she is more predisposed to accept. But his advice to 'Begin with … / The sacrament of marriage' (lines 304–5) is not without a rueful coda and is in strange agreement with the Cardinal's, who thinks the sacramental institution a prison. Antonio concludes there is no middle way. Marriage 'contains or heaven, or hell' (line 313).

But for Antonio, the real devil is ambition. Fear of it, as a wise counsellor, slows his natural inclination towards a growing intimacy and delays the wooing. Because, however clever or learned or educated a counsellor is, he knows that marrying nobility will be fiercely resisted; because of a dilution of property, or power, or simply pride. So she must claim him with 'but half a blush'. He can only offer 'the constant sanctuary / Of your good name' (lines 376–7), not his. She is, and will remain, the Duchess of Malfi still.

The mellifluous but subtle **alliteration** Antonio uses cloaks the insidious nature of ambition. 'Ambition, Madam, is a great man's madness' (line 337). As the play develops we will witness how ambition makes one man a 'lunatic, beyond all cure' (line 341) and corrupts the integrity of others.

2 **partaker of the natures** knowledgeable of character

159 **cozens** deceives

220 **Laban's sheep** biblical reference to Jacob's relative whose animals were diseased

274 **ingenious** frank

289 **tane** taken

ACT II

SCENE 1 **Bosola's disdain for decadence is followed by his rejection of an accusation of ambition. He offers the Duchess apricots, which she eagerly accepts. The fruit brings on a sudden illness which Antonio fears is the onset of labour, and therefore the exposure of their secret**

Bosola becomes Castruchio's bully. The courtier's old age and delusions are the focus of Bosola's mockery. An old lady, perhaps the midwife, passes by and causes him to muse about the Duchess's health and the decadence of the court, 'A rotten and dead body / ... in rich tissue' (lines 60–1).

The Duchess enters complaining of being out of condition and is little kinder to her old lady attendant about her foul breath than was Bosola about her foul looks. The Duchess's petulance is a nice show of fallibility. The way she eats the apricots, Bosola suspects, demonstrates a gluttony associated with pregnancy. Antonio seems too anxious (and too inexperienced?) to enter into the banter of **double entendres** that runs between the Duchess and Bosola. She complains of feeling unwell and Antonio fears she has gone into labour without the opportunity of concealing her condition.

Bosola's characteristics as **malcontent** and bitter wit come to the fore. Ambition, again, is the topic of conversation between Bosola, whose tendency is to bully, and Castruchio, who tendency is towards senility.

Antonio has seen ambition as something to be avoided, Castruchio as something to embrace; he would like to be President of the criminal court. Bosola mocks the features deemed important for the job. The discussion adds to the picture of a corrupt and indisciplined court and state. Bosola caps this comic episode with a prophetic comment 'I will teach a trick …' (line 20). He is and will be full of 'tricks', not just the one he confides he has in line 72.

The old lady who interrupts them is perhaps a retired servant of the Duchess. Certainly she features in that sort of capacity later in the scene. She isn't spared Bosola's vitriol. He is scandalously offensive about her looks, dismisses her and the old man to adultery, seeing them as the end result of the corruption he rails so vehemently against.

Antonio and Delio bring each other and the audience up to date; an authorial device particularly useful when there have been significant time gaps between scenes, as here. Bosola slips from being the tormentor to being their butt. His bon mot 'For the subtlest / folly proceeds from the subtlest wisdom' (lines 82–3) may be behind Delio's much later observation of his being a 'fantastical scholar' (III.3.40).

Bosola has to remind himself that his spymaster Ferdinand expects melancholia of him as well as cunning. To Antonio's admonition to refrain from an untypical gloominess comes Bosola's subdued rejoinder 'a lawyer's mule of a slow pace / will both suit my disposition and business' (lines 93–4). Given the protracted time it takes him to gather 'intelligence' this **dramatic irony** is a joke against his own profession that lawyer Webster could not resist.

Bosola is better at deriding than flattery. So his praise of Antonio for being 'chief man / with the Duchess' (lines 99–100) is tinged with the contempt the low-born reserve for the high-born, 'the same reason, that / makes a vicar go to law for a tithe-pig' (lines 107–8).

Pregnancy changes the Duchess. She is less focused, more petulant, intolerant and distracted by fashion. Antonio becomes a paler person in her presence. Bosola seizes the opportunity for his 'trick' and offers her apricots. Perhaps there is a reversal here of an Edenic echo. It is 'Adam' who offers 'Eve' the forbidden fruit. Early-season and force-ripened in horse dung (another image of corruption), it will bring on her labour and betrayal.

As he feeds his mistress's greed, Bosola engages with **metaphors** of fecundity; how fruit that is grafted is better than the original. Note the **pun**. Grafting is his slow uncovering of truth; what she is up to, too; he knows she is pregnant, in a fruitful state. He would know, but doesn't, how she got into it.

It has become night. Antonio panics. Delio coolly checks out the birth arrangements and prepares the alibis. The courtier is counsellor now.

25 **face physic** face make-up
113 **litter** an enclosed coach
139 **pare** peel

SCENE 2 **Bosola's spying is frustrated and he finds himself caught up in Antonio's stratagem to maintain secrecy about the birth of a son. Bosola is detained under suspicion of theft**

Bosola's earlier 'abusing women' works against him. The old lady refuses to discuss the Duchess's 'apparent signs / of breeding' (lines 3–4) with him. Antonio enters and orders that the gates be shut by Forobosco who, although appearing on the cast list, has the singular distinction of having no words to speak and no stage-entry to make. The servants think the curfew has been imposed because a guard has been found in the Duchess's bedchamber 'with a pistol in his great cod-piece' (line 37).

Antonio orders that everyone be confined to their rooms pending a search for apparently missing jewels. Delio quietens Antonio's anxiety and prepares to leave for Rome, assuring him 'Old friends, like old swords, still are trusted best' (line 75). Cariola brings in a baby and Antonio hurries off to have his new-born son's horoscope revealed.

The 'old lady' is in haste. Perhaps she is the midwife and can renew usefulness to the Duchess. Perhaps she was wet-nurse to the Duchess in her infancy. At any rate, her enhanced status gives her the opportunity to put Bosola in his place. She ignores his saucy **innuendo**, 'The lusty spring smells well: but drooping autumn / tastes well' (lines 17–18). Her chance to snub him must be deeply satisfying given his recent disparagement of her, his equal, and old Castruchio, very much his social superior. Bosola returns to the theme of counselling but somehow sounds lame in the face of her new-found confidence.

Antonio has recovered his poise and is doing his best to secure the Duchess's secret. He is not below a cunning ploy himself, spreading a rumour that his mistress's poisoning necessitates the palace gates be locked. Effectively the Duchess is imprisoned along with her officers whilst a search takes place for a trumped-up theft. **Ironically**, the only jewellery that has changed hands so far in the play has been to Antonio, a diamond for good horsemanship and a ring from his wife.

Bosola and two servants indulge in ribald gossip: how a Swiss guard has been found in a sexually compromising act in the Duchess's bedchamber. Their kind of barrack-room **innuendo** gives us a strong indication of where Bosola's place is in the hierarchy.

In this respect the text adds something to performance. The lines lower-order characters speak, for instance Bosola in the opening scene of the play, are usually in **prose**; only upper-class roles and more significant speeches are dignified by verse. The convention allows, however, that when the lower orders are engaged in quick-fire dialogue the playwright may lighten the moment by employing **blank verse** again.

26 **girdle** belt
29 **posterns** back doors

SCENE 3   Antonio and Bosola are both on clandestine spying
          missions and a chance night-time meeting brings their
          mutual hostility into the open. Antonio drops the new
          baby's horoscope and after he has gone Bosola wastes no
          time in communicating the paper's information back to
          Rome

Bosola sees Antonio's restricting order as a means of concealment and
inhibiting his commission. They meet creeping around the grounds, both
hearing a cry from the Duchess's chamber. Squaring up to each other,
Bosola implies Antonio is nervous and Antonio challenges Bosola's
breaking bounds. Antonio suggests that Bosola has poisoned the Duchess,
an accusation anticipated in II.2.34. They trade insults of a more personal
nature, Antonio for once being as blunt as the 'saucy slave' Bosola.

  Antonio's agitation culminates in a spontaneous nose-bleed. He
pulls a cloth from his pocket to staunch the blood, inadvertently dropping
the baby's horoscope. Bosola picks the paper up surreptitiously and
discovers that the Duchess has just delivered a child, its paternity a
mystery. He will send Castruchio, eager anyway to further his ambitions,
to Rome with information of this birth.

  Bosola hears 'a woman shriek' (line 1). This seems to be a flashback
  in time, or a Webster 'error' as the baby's birth was announced by
  Cariola in the previous scene. Bosola tries to undermine Antonio's
  position, first insinuating himself as a 'friend' (line 13), and then as
  equal servants flouting the Duchess's strict instructions to keep to
  their quarters.

  Antonio quickly recovers, again employing deception in order to
  menace Bosola accused of being 'a night-walker' (line 25). Bosola is
  aggrieved at Antonio's pulling rank and responds the only way he
  knows, with insolence. There is **irony** in their traded insults. Bosola
  calls Antonio 'a false steward' (line 35) which indeed he is; he is the
  Duchess's husband disguised as a steward. And Antonio has already
  imputed Bosola is a traitor. Tragically, that is exactly what he has
  become.

  Antonio leaves with his nose-bleed, not a happy reminder of Delio's
  litany of omens in the previous scene, 'How superstitiously we

mind our evils! / ... / Bleeding at nose, the stumbling of a horse'
(II.2.68, 70).

Bosola, still loose from his lodgings, is bereft of any 'friend' except
a 'false' one, the lantern which gave away his presence to Antonio
in the first place. But luck is with him because of the lantern after
all. On the ground is the new baby's horoscope.

Either the prophecy is wrong or Webster has made a 'slip'. The
paper 'signifies short life ... a violent death' (lines 61–3). This baby
will, in fact, survive the play; to be presented at its end as the
Duchess's heir. But let us give the benefit to Webster. He could
have intended, in a play so full of deceit, for the paper 'of nativity'
to mislead.

1 **list** listen

65 **bawd** similar to pander, pimp, derogatory word for 'sexual' messenger with
effeminate connotations

SCENE 4   **The Cardinal's pillow-talk with his mistress is both witty
and cold. Delio, newly arrived in Rome, is not so witty
and attempts to regain past favours from Julia. She hears
that her husband has also come from Amalfi**

In Rome, and probably in bed, is the Cardinal with his mistress.
Corruption has the upper hand and there are uncanny parallels between
the passionless Cardinal and his passionate sister.

The titillating intimacy of Julia with her 'anchorite' (line 4) is the
playwright's light relief after Antonio's palpable anxiety. The Cardinal
calls her 'witty false' (line 5), an **oxymoronic** and meretricious paradox
typically characteristic of the superficiality of their circle. She half
accuses him of inconstancy, which he turns back on her as adulterous
wife, adamant that all women are unreliable. To her tears he adds, and
demands, kisses, and proudly proclaims his prowess as a lover.

Their 'play' is interrupted by a servant, announcing that Delio
wishes to see her, and that 'old Castruchio' (line 44) has arrived in Rome.
The Cardinal withdraws. Delio enters. She is only just out of the
Cardinal's arms. But Delio is a former lover. Seeing her dressed for bed
inflames his old desire for her. He makes fun of her husband though he

himself is a clumsy and impatient wooer. He offers to become her banker.

She is more than a match for him and asks what conditions attach to his money. He demeans himself further by levelling her to an object of quantifiable worth. She is not impressed. Delio is however spared further humiliation by the servant with further news of Julia's husband, who has delivered a letter to Ferdinand which has put the Duke 'out of his wits' (line 69), a madness soon to become more publicly apparent.

Julia halts the banter with Delio, but not before he asks her to be his mistress. She says she will ask permission. Delio remains bemused as to her intentions and concerned as to Antonio's safety.

Webster starts another scene with a trick, this time Julia's subterfuge in coming to the Cardinal in Rome. Paradoxically she tells the truth to live a lie; she has come to visit a holy man (which he should be but isn't), 'for devotion' (which she displays to him which he cannot display to God) (line 5).

He rejects her charge of inconstancy with male logic, challenging female consistency. It is easier to make glass malleable than find a constant woman, he suggests. More likely to view for a constant woman on another world than find one here.

He will not be compromised by her tears either. He, like Bosola, is into animal **imagery** but less skilful in its use. He has rescued her from a 'melancholy perch' (line 28) like a game bird, 'Like a tame elephant' (line 32). In fact theirs is a relationship to which he, her handler, feels very little commitment because he is incapable of much feeling anyway. Describing pervasive irreligion at court, Webster demystifies religion and robs it of its power.

Most critics compare the coldness of this liaison with the passion of Antonio and the Duchess's. But both the Cardinal and his sister are in intimate relationships which are disruptive and which thrive on deceit.

Julia has been humiliated by the Cardinal. Her spirit is restored by the renewed attentions of an old lover. He may prove alternative fun, the third man (and not the last) with whom she will 'associate' in the play. She enters into Delio's suggestiveness enthusiastically.

Confidence in Antonio is further undermined by his association with such an amoral friend. Shortcomings of character displayed here are a far cry from those qualities so much admired in the Duchess. Antonio has shown he can lie to escape trouble. Now Delio is ready to buy sex as a distraction from idleness.

1 **prithee** colloquial for 'pray thee'

4 **anchorite** religious hermit or recluse

26 **cuckold** husband to unfaithful wife

42 **post** postillion

56 **breach** trouser

SCENE 5   **The Aragon brothers anguish over their sister. Ferdinand's accusations grow wilder. The Cardinal loses patience with such extreme views. The Duke calms, assuming for a while an attitude of sleep**

Bosola's letter, together with the horoscope, is discussed by the Duchess's brothers. Ferdinand becomes increasingly unrestrained in his anger to a point where the Cardinal, initially sympathetic, complains that he flies beyond reason.

Whether the mandrake is the letter, the baby or his thoughts, some narcotic is certainly poisoning the roots of Ferdinand's imagination. He says their sister is unchaste with a dagger (penis?) up to the hilt, i.e. as far as she possibly can be. Furthermore, he claims, she has been flagrantly promiscuous. He tells the Cardinal that he can even see her 'in the shameful act of sin' (line 41). These are the words of a frustrated voyeur. He debases himself by debasing her, his vivid imagination taking him into debauched fantasy.

The Cardinal has had enough. Ferdinand persists, suggesting that the sin is theirs. It must be expunged. Killing her is not enough. She must be destroyed, and her child must be boiled to a meat broth.

'Are you stark mad?' (line 67) asks the hastily withdrawing Cardinal. Ferdinand immediately regains self-control. He will 'sleep' until he knows 'who leaps my sister' (line 78). That known …

Why should Ferdinand become so incensed? Amalfi is not part of the Aragon family's inheritance. The Duchess's territory comes to her in trust for her son by her first marriage from her deceased husband. Perhaps his anger lies in her disregard of his strong counsel (a theme that threads its way through the play) not to marry, or more significantly because Ferdinand harbours incestuous and unfulfilled intentions.

Ferdinand's language seems insanely intemperate, bordering on the pornographic. Folklore likens a mandrake to a man, its root a sexual organ. Dig it up, and the accompanying shriek has redolences of the birth experience, immediately poignant in the news just received about the baby. The Duke has dug up the information; he tells his brother that he would like to dig up the whole incident.

Digging up a mandrake was thought to lead to insanity, and Ferdinand knows his perversion is sick. 'I am grown mad with't' (line 2). He brands his sister a prostitute. It cannot be that his family pride has been besmirched by her loss of virginity – she has already had two children by her first husband. By branding her degenerate he conceals his jealous lust.

His expressions of anger, his strong accusations, his railing against the weakness of women, begin to win over a Cardinal who himself has only recently uttered the same sentiments about his mistress.

But Ferdinand's outbursts trouble the Cardinal, who knows this to be the kind of dangerous anger which deforms judgement. He signals his imminent departure. All at once, Ferdinand is spent. His sister has slept with a garrison, his brother sleeps with Julia, and he will 'go sleep' too. It will be lonely, much of it in an unreal world and will culminate in the final sleep of death.

25 **cupping-glass** surgical instrument used to draw blood by suction, vacuum caused by heat
34 **bark** small boat
59 **chide** rebuke
60 **divers** different, various
68 **ventage** air-hole

ACT III

SCENE 1   Two more children have been born to the Duchess.
Antonio and Delio bring each other up to date.
Ferdinand's visit to Amalfi is causing unease because of
his uncharacteristic peaceableness. He calms the
Duchess's fears by seeming to accept her rejection of his
choice of a husband for her, as well as his rejection of
court rumour about her. Alone with Bosola, the Duke
extracts a key to her room, intending to extract a
confession from his sister

Delio returns to Malfi in the company of Delio and learns of Antonio's growing family. The action of the play must have moved on at least eighteen months (unless the children are twins). The friends exchange news.

Antonio expresses a fear that the Duchess's brothers must know of her childbearing. Ferdinand's peacefulness is worrying, 'He is so quiet / … Those houses that are haunted, are most still, / Till the devil be up' (lines 21–4).

He is concerned too with the Duchess's public reputation and of the jaded opinion of even the wiser heads at court in believing he is bettering himself at the Duchess's expense, unaware of their married status.

The Duchess, the Duke and Bosola join the two friends. Webster now constructs an elaborate **dramatic irony** to be played out by Ferdinand. The Duke plans a husband for the Duchess. We know what he does not; that she already has a husband. Ferdinand knows what the Duchess does not; that he is aware that she already has a lover who has given her at least one child. And we know that Antonio does not know whether the Duke knows or not that she now has those two further children! The playwright weaves his web of deceit and the audience looks forward to a slow and tragic resolution.

The Duchess discounts the possibility of a marriage with Malateste, a mere count, heaping on further **irony** by saying that when she does marry it will be for the Duke's honour. She adds that whilst discussing family values she would like to raise an associated matter with her brother, that of the rumours going about the court which impinge on *her* honour. He dismisses such rumours as the stuff of court. 'Go, be safe / In your own innocency' (lines 54–5). Which is exactly what he believes she cannot be.

Bosola is left with Ferdinand, who asks for an intelligence update. Bosola passes on a mix of fact, rumour and his own uncertainty. The Duke decides it is time he took the initiative, to 'force confession from her' (line 79). He asks Bosola for the duplicate key to his sister's bedchamber. His private purposes are beyond understanding, he intimates presciently.

Bosola cannot resist another insult, attributing self-flattery to the Duke. Ferdinand's response is mild, commending Bosola for being the first in his pay not to indulge in flattery, ending in a couplet of false complicity stressing the need of the great to have a friend who is straight.

Antonio and Delio tease each other about their respective appearances. Antonio looks leaner from the increased responsibilities of parenthood, Delio is blissfully single.

Antonio reports that Ferdinand is dangerously quiet. He 'seems to sleep' (line 21); what the Duke told his brother he would do. Antonio also reports the unease of the Duchess's courtiers at her burgeoning family and his increasing wealth.

Ferdinand enters, on his way to bed; which reminds him about a suitor for his sister. She suggests that the count selected would not improve the Duke's good name, the **irony** being that she is already married to a person of even lesser status.

Ferdinand dismisses her concern about court gossip. Perhaps he has already heard of her 'reputation'. He has no wish to alarm her prematurely into caution.

Alone with Bosola, talk turns to the Duchess's bastard children. He gives no credence to Bosola's suggestion that she is a hapless victim of sorcery.

Bosola fixes on her significant undoing, that she has married and kept it secret. We may have sympathy with such a view. She has married despite her earlier protestations to Antonio to 'put off all vain ceremony' (I.2.372). Bosola suggests that Ferdinand's uncovering of her secret is like 'bawdy aphrodisiacs' (see Note to

line 75 in the New Mermaid edition) which make 'the patient mad'
(line 76). We are left to conjecture who the patient is.

The Duke demands the key to his sister's bed-chamber he had
earlier commissioned Bosola to obtain. It is handed over minus
flattery and plus impudence. Flattery is a major theme. Ferdinand
admits he is surrounded by its practitioners. He pretends to
recognise Bosola as a friend, a hollow concept for a **malcontent**
who once tried himself for such a status with Antonio.

6 **pedigree** person's line of descent
14 **reversion** position or property remaining after estate's disposal
70 **gulleries** deceptions
71 **mountebanks** tricksters, cheats, impostors
84 **drifts** tendencies, intents, aims
93 **rails** regulates, puts right, brings back to order

SCENE 2   **The night begins with happy intimacy and ends with
fearful destiny. Antonio and the Duchess decide to 'sleep'
together despite the close proximity of Ferdinand. Whilst
Antonio and Cariola engage in childish play, Ferdinand
enters unannounced, leaving soon after in fury for Rome.
The Duchess plans Antonio's escape to Ancona, to join
him there soon. She confides in Bosola that Antonio is
father to their three children, and asks him to convey her
wealth to her husband. Bosola is relieved that his wretched
task of serving opposing masters is nearly complete**

The action now moves to the heart of Amalfi, the Duchess's palace,
her bed-chamber. Good-natured intercourse ensues over plans for night-
time frolics, tempered by a need for furtiveness in view of the lurking
danger Ferdinand's proximity compels; 'Love mix'd with fear is sweetest'
(line 66).

Antonio and the Duchess's pre-pillow talk is a more lively
passion than their earlier nuptials, or that of the Cardinal and Julia. As
they prepare for bed, Antonio suggests a game of hide-and-seek to
Cariola. The Duchess, unaware of their absence, is talking as Ferdinand
steals in, holding the dagger he did when first he warned her not to
remarry.

She invites her brother to kill her. But he is a schemer of violence, not a practitioner, and invites her to kill herself. She confesses she is married, albeit not nobly. He can hardly bear to look at her let alone hear her speak. He is sure her lover is within earshot and bitterly suggests he 'would have thee build / Such a room for him, as our anchorites / To holier use inhabit' (lines 102–4) to protect them both from the violence he feels.

Ferdinand leaves her with a moralistic fable, saying he will not see her again. Antonio and Cariola furtively return, in a state of high anxiety. Antonio demonstrates a flawed nature, adding to superficiality cowardice and instability by pointing a gun at Cariola and accusing her of treachery.

The Duchess constructs a series of subterfuges to secure her family's safety. Antonio boasts he will fight back if Ferdinand returns but meanwhile leaves to plan his escape. Bosola arrives to announce the peremptory departure of Ferdinand to Rome.

She knows that only escape from Malfi can save her family and plans to accuse Antonio by 'a noble lie' (line 180) of dishonest dealings and have him expelled. She summons her staff, Antonio's old ploy. Bosola exits, thinking he sees cunning in this. Antonio returns, but the Duchess has too little time to finalise rendezvous arrangements before Bosola and the household servants reappear to hear the steward exiled.

Antonio flees, condemned by the household except Bosola who, in tirading against 'intelligencers' and flatterers, himself flatters Antonio as 'an honest statesman' (line 262). To the Duchess's ears this is 'excellent music' (line 274). She cannot refrain from confiding in Bosola that Antonio is her husband.

In one moment Bosola achieves by luck all that the years of patient deceit have not. He dare not now lose his prize. So he praises his mistress for preferring 'A man merely for worth' (line 278). He vows he will keep her confidence and is promptly made custodian of her wealth.

Bosola suggests that instead of going to Ancona she should pilgrimage to Loretto. The Duchess ignores Cariola's objection to feigned pilgrimages, dubbing her 'a superstitious fool' (line 317).

In disregarding Cariola's religious scruples and suggested alternative of fleeing to Germany, the Duchess passes up an opportunity of putting herself outside her brothers' jurisdiction. Bosola is left to contemplate his task of 'intelligencer', to 'reveal / All to my lord' (lines 324–5). Despised he may be, but 'rais'd' and 'prais'd' (lines 328, 329) he will be.

This long scene is pivotal, marking the beginning of the Duchess's demise and a setting for the **sophistry** of those ranged against her.

On their way to bed the Duchess seduces her husband as 'a lord of mis-rule' (line 7), an appropriate **double entendre** not only because such was the title given to the master of ceremonies of night-time revels but because Malfi seems to be a place and Antonio a person constantly on the edge of dysfunction.

He seems increasingly ineffective and dull, responding to the Duchess's mischievous suggestions with a heavy banality. Cariola joins in the fun with a naughty **pun** 'Wherefore still, when you lie with my lady / Do you rise so early?' (lines 17–18) to which he can only mumble that he associates himself with 'Labouring men' (line 18). Later he adds faintheartedness to his dreariness.

By contrast, the Duchess sparkles. Before, she had suggested they 'lay a naked sword between us, keep us chaste' (I.2.414). Now she complains that 'sleeping' has no pleasure for lovers. He attempts badinage, but it is blunt compared with the women's wit.

The coquettish **tone** evaporates with Ferdinand's surreptitious entry. As soon as she sees him the Duchess knows she has given herself away. She is ready for the consequences and responds with the dignity she instinctively feels a prince should publicly display.

Ferdinand hands her the family dagger, inviting her to follow honour and kill herself. Bosola also once offered her a knife, to pare the apricots, and she refused that one then. She refuses Ferdinand's now.

She tells him she is married; not to his liking, but still, she would like to introduce him to her husband. After all, she reasons, Ferdinand could hardly have entered her room without Antonio's consent.

The Duke silences her with a savage depravity. He will no more meet her 'lecher' than he would kill the screech-owl he perceives her to be. His tirade echoes Julia's excuse to Castruchio 'to visit an old anchorite' (II.4.4), and seems a long remove from his promise to his brother to sleep until he has discovered who 'leaps my sister' (II.5.78), or indeed his promise to her to be deaf to any rumours about her.

She tries more reasoning. Why not marry? Because, Ferdinand declares, she has been married already. The implication is that marrying again would be bigamous, someone marrying her would be adulterous, and their children would be bastards. She has disobeyed (the sin of Adam and Eve), fouled Ferdinand's reputation and sullied his image of her; by implication, allowed another man to take his place.

He tells her a fable about Reputation, Love and Death. She has said goodbye to Reputation, of which he sees himself a personification, and now he says a final goodbye to her in her defiant refusal to be cased up 'like a holy relic' (line 139). Denigration of relics as idolatrous by a playwright is popular with Puritan audiences.

Webster is also concerned with corruption at King James's court. Open criticism however would be a dangerous course. Italy, and specifically Rome, and its courts thus become perfect surrogates, centres of culture but otherwise as alien, hostile, seedbeds of corruption and, in particular, Catholic corruption.

The scene's third episode is brief. Antonio and Cariola re-enter to ascertain how hazardous things have become. They need to act fast. Bosola comes with news of the Duke's hasty departure to Rome, and that they are 'undone' (line 165). Quick is the Duchess's retort 'Indeed, I am very near it' (line 165). She is undressed, ready to bed Antonio, and in flagrant disobedience of her brother's wishes. She must find a way to banish him to save them all.

The scene's fourth section uses short emphatic sentences to heighten tension. The Duchess outlines her plan to Antonio, emphasising her device's 'weak safety / Runs upon enginous wheels: short syllables / Must stand for periods' (lines 176–8).

Bosola enters with court officers. They butt in on Antonio's stage-managed dismissal and defence, composed of **dramatic ironies**. She confiscates his wealth. He responds 'I am all yours; and 'tis very fit / All mine should be so' (lines 205–6). She dismisses him, and his **irony** is laid on irony 'You may see, gentlemen, what 'tis to serve / A prince with body and soul' (lines 208–9).

In the final episode, the sixth scene within this scene, the Duchess prolongs the charade by asking her staff's opinion of her disgraced steward. They variously denounce him, and depart. Left alone with Bosola, she seeks his opinion of her staff. He denounces them as flatterers and praises Antonio as 'too honest' (line 243), even if, as she complains, and as he may consider ruefully applies the more to himself, 'he was basely descended' (line 258).

By contrast he refers to Antonio as a prince and predicts 'You shall want him' (line 261), likening him to a 'cedar, planted by a spring' (line 263), differing markedly from his former description of the princely Aragon brothers who were 'like plum trees, that grow / crooked over standing pools' (I.1.49–50); the cedar, tall and straight and fed by fresh water, the plum trees squat and crooked and drawing nourishment from over-ripe stagnation.

Whether dissembling like the staff, or being contrarily frank, Bosola's empathetic strategy works in drawing her on and, in a fatal moment of weakness, she confides he is talking about her husband. Bosola keeps up his act. In identifying a new-found confidante she misses picking up on his flattery.

Slipping into the role of counsellor he suggests Loretto as a preferable goal for the fugitives to Ancona. She can go there under the guise of pilgrimage. Cariola, does not approve of pilgrimage as disguise and thinks of a secular excuse for the journey; a spa in the northern hills, or Germany.

Bosola is alarmed by this suggestion. He may despise his role of intelligencer but his puzzle is solved and reward is within his grasp. He knows the identity of his quarries and their planned movements. He must keep in touch until his masters have them all in the bag.

His fears are groundless. The Duchess rejects her maid's good counsel for his. He is trusted with the last penny of her wealth which he knows she will never see again; a great deal more, too, than he could ever expect from the Duke or the Cardinal.

41 **benight the apprehension** blur understanding

45 **hard favour'd** unattractive

55 **divers** often

56 **chaf'd** become furious

59 **wax** grow

89 **By his confederacy** near his union or contract; sometimes conspiracy, thus the words have connotations of secrecy

101 **lecher** lover

108 **paraquito** parrot

149 **warrantable** justifiable

154 **rank gall** foul intestine, therefore loathsome

160 **part** depart

187 ***Quietus*** receipt discharging debts due

193 **publish** make public

202 **loth** unwilling

214–15 **pig's head gaping … find him a Jew** Two proverbs brought together: Jews are forbidden by religious law to have anything to do with pigs or pork

219 **black wool** an old cure for deafness

220 **thick** sick

247 **post** fast, express

    scuttles rapid runs

283 **unbenific'd** unsupported (financially)

306 **feign** pretend

307 **leagues** one league is a distance of about five kilometres

324 **rests** remains

329 **weeds, to the life** mundane matters, with verisimilitude

SCENE 3 The Cardinal turns soldier and Ferdinand and then Bosola arrive in Rome to plan the Duchess's banishment from Ancona

Bosola in Rome finds the Cardinal caught up in preparations for war. Discussion at court centres on the unmanly Malateste, suggested by the

Duke as a suitable match for the Duchess and rejected by her as 'a mere stick of sugar-candy' (III.1.42).

Talk turns to corruption in the church, and to Bosola's closeting with the Aragon brothers. Delio, here, to defend Antonio, describes Bosola as a 'fantastical scholar' (line 40), a 'speculative man' (line 46), by implication full of theory, a would-be academic sidetracked by detail.

The brothers' agitation is noted; in particular Ferdinand's hysterical laugh. We listen in to their dialogue in which they damn their sister's superficial attitude to religion, and make plans for her banishment. Of Antonio they are dismissive, 'A slave that only smell'd of ink and counters' (line 71).

> Gossip dominates. The Cardinal sloughs off religious pretence for a more comfortable secularism and Malateste panders to his militaristic aspirations, 'The Emperor, / Hearing your worth that way, ere you attain'd / This reverend garment, joins you in commission' (lines 1–3).
>
> Malateste goes unrewarded. Delio, of lost reputation, sides with those who disparage Malateste as effete and effeminate.
>
> Delio defines Bosola, whom he formerly knew, as 'a fantastical scholar', a characteristic of the **malcontent** the audience will be unfamiliar with. Delio refers to Bosola's eye for detail, perhaps with a notion that it is Bosola that has brought such trouble to the Duchess's court.
>
> Pescara joins the disparagers, blaming the bickering cardinals for creating chaos. He comments on Ferdinand's deadly unpredictability and Silvio adds that the Cardinal is like 'a foul porpoise before a storm' (line 52).
>
> Meanwhile, Ferdinand is indulging in another character assassination, of Antonio 'A slave, that only smell'd of ink and counters'. The audience may be rapidly coming to a similar conclusion.

10 **muster book** a book for registering military personnel

28 **pate** head, particularly where the intellect was said to be located

29 **pot-gun** pop-gun, a child's wooden toy

_46_ **speculative** implications of double-mindedness

_70_ **honesty** chastity (or lack of it!)

SCENE 4 Two pilgrims at Loretto comment on the Cardinal's transformation from priest to soldier. In dumb-show, the Duchess and her family are banished from Ancona. Questions are posed about the whole legality of these proceedings against her

The shrine in Loretto, in preference to Ancona, is where Bosola has persuaded the Duchess to meet Antonio. Two pilgrims commentate on the Cardinal removing his episcopal garb to don the uniform of a soldier.

It is reasonable to question how dumb the dumb-show is. Throughout, there is music and song. Antonio, the Duchess and her family present themselves at the shrine. The pilgrims are surprised the Duchess has married so beneath herself, but are disapproving of the Cardinal's harshness and question the legality of the Duchess's banishment. They observe cynically that church and state are equally free of the law, and conclude by recounting the Cardinal's injustice in seizing the Duchess's wedding ring, a 'sacrifice / To his revenge' (lines 37–8).

Throughout the scene, a sycophantic song is heard.

Authorship of parts of this scene are dubious; particularly the abysmal couplets that form the heart of its text but are all but irrelevant to the heart of its matter. Irrelevant because the key dilemmas are: by what justice and by what authority?

The lords of Aragon have no authority in Malfi, ruled by the Duchess as regent by reason of her first marriage on behalf of her first infant son. But we are far from Amalfi, in the heartland of the Aragon brothers influence.

Webster uses dispassionate observers to describe the silent action played out before them. This play-within-a-play is common in the drama of the period. It encourages the audience into distancing, and gives relief from the preceding intensity. T.S. Eliot disapproved of **Renaissance** dramatists who attempted 'to attain complete realism without surrendering unrealistic conventions'.

What the pilgrims watch is wholly poignant; a nuclear family relegated to a passive role, and a priest converting back to being a soldier.

The two groups are related but show no filial affection. They pass as if on an escalator, one going up and one going down, both looking unseeingly ahead.

The pilgrims ponder crassnesses so beyond the boundaries of reason; a 'great lady ... match'd herself / Unto so mean a person' (lines 24–5) and a priest who 'resigns his cardinal's hat', bearing 'himself much too cruel' (line 26). The violence of family hate, and justice set too easily aside.

6 **dumb-show** play without speech

SCENE 5   **The Duchess is overtaken by Bosola who has come from Ferdinand to demand that Antonio report on a business matter. Bosola leaves with a refusal. The Duchess divides her group by sending Antonio on to Milan with their eldest son. Bosola returns, disguised, to put the Duchess into the 'protection' of her brothers and return her to house arrest in Malfi. She submits, realising this may be the beginning of the end for her, still harbouring hope**

Banished, in flight, the Duchess and her family discuss the gloomy future. Bosola overtakes them with a letter of phoney reassurance from Ferdinand, 'like to calm weather / At sea before a tempest, false hearts speak fair / To those they intend most mischief' (lines 24–6). The letter confirms her suspicions, 'Send Antonio to me; I want his head in a business' (line 27). Head, not counsel, she observes.

The letter refers to debts incurred by Antonio in Naples; hardly surprising, seeing that Bosola was present previously when the Duchess concocted her steward's 'banishment' for dealing 'so falsely ... / My brother stood engag'd with me for money / Ta'ne up of certain Neapolitan Jews, / And Antonio lets the bonds be forfeit' (III.2.167–70). Ferdinand ends his letter ominously. 'I had rather have his heart than his / money (lines 34–5).' Heart not money, she observes.

The Duchess sees through these riddles. She and Antonio refuse to submit, he asserting that these demands come from 'brothers' (line 47), a claim to kinship Bosola mocks. The **irony** is that if Antonio's breeding is base, and his kinship with the Duke is admitted, then Ferdinand, by association, is included in Bosola's definition, in line with what we already knows is Bosola's opinion of the princely brothers!

Bosola parts with an ominous promise to return. Antonio asserts that it is the Duchess who is now the counsellor. He quickly submits to leaving her to her fate, substituting platitudes for passion in their parting kiss and causing her to liken it to one an anchorite would give a skull. Antonio breathtakingly exhorts her to save 'your little ones ... / from the tiger' (lines 82–83). By the Duchess's **tone** we know she thinks this is a final severance.

Antonio gone, Bosola reappears disguised. The Duchess seems relieved that her waiting is over, 'I would have my ruin / Be sudden' (lines 94–5). Bosola is to place her under house-arrest in Malfi, her brothers having acted for her 'safety and pity' (line 107); pity, one half of **tragedy**! She is 'arm'd 'gainst misery' (line 141), and answers with spirit that although her children are too young to talk, yet their first words will be curses. Bosola urges her to forget the low-born Antonio, and she retorts that, had she the strength, she would fight with more than words. The riddle she recounts is capped by an aphorism, 'Men oft are valued high, when th'are most wretch'd' (line 140). She recognises she is midway between fatalism and optimism, 'There's no deep valley, but near some great hill' (line 143).

> Like all displaced persons down on their luck the Duchess finds that most of her retinue has melted away. As they flee along a road to nowhere, she muses 'They have done wisely' (line 6) to cut and run. She dreams of diamonds turned to pearls and communicates her gloom to Antonio, who sees those pearls as tears.

> The Duchess thinks birds are an apt **metaphor** for marriage, 'Happier than we; for they may choose their mates' (line 19). But she chose her mate and it has brought her her present unhappiness.

> Motive is a powerful theme in this scene. Bosola, nervous that his quarry may get away, catches up with the bedraggled group. He uses all his cunning to bring his mission to fruition; he must bring them all to book, the Duchess, her lover and their bastard children.

> The Duchess is sceptical about the 'safety' (line 23) she is offered. She knows her brothers, knows their motives, 'like to

calm weather / At sea before a tempest, false hearts speak fair / To those they intend most mischief'. She has little difficulty in discerning and rejecting their subterfuge. She intends to keep Antonio's head and heart from her brother's clutches.

Antonio chooses to remain and protect/endanger the Duchess rather than face Ferdinand, a cowardice which disgusts Bosola, 'This proclaims your breeding. / Every small thing draws a base mind to fear' (lines 51–2). Of course, Bosola and Ferdinand mean Antonio no good. But his feebleness is nonetheless disappointing.

As the spirit of her consort wanes the Duchess's waxes. She assumes new moral stature. Bosola has no sooner turned away than she banishes Antonio for the second time with their oldest son towards Milan, the direction she now knows they should have gone the first time on Cariola's advice. The Duchess is about to lose her counsellor and so reverses the role and counsels him.

She adopts a stoicism about their imminent parting, approving their son's cheerful innocence in a miserable world, where mature understanding only brings sorrow.

Discourse grows increasingly stilted. Antonio is both trite and noble. Despite the menace to both of them, he thinks he is the one in danger.

The Duchess complains of her husband's coldness, like 'an holy anchorite'. She wants a warmer goodbye. Cold distancing, of course, is a male coping strategy.

As soon as Antonio, personification of heaviness, is gone, Bosola reappears, just as the Duchess knew he would. It is as if he watched until Antonio went, then pounced. Contrary to Antonio's presumption, the Duchess is Bosola's business, to prevent this 'silly bird' (his **metaphor** for her) being caught in Antonio's nets. The **irony** is that he is freeing her from the net of marriage to put her into the even more recognisable net of house arrest.

She sees returning to Malfi as a one-way passage. Bosola attempts to persuade her to forget her 'low fellow' of a husband, a far cry from his earlier extravagant praise, 'Let me show you what a most unvalu'd jewel / You have, in a wanton humour, thrown away' (III.2.248-9).

Her response is one of the great speeches of the play, applying the fable of the salmon and the dogfish emphasising that a first demonstration of strength is no indicator of end-worth.

  2 **train** attendants, followers
  5 **buntings** birds similar to sparrows or finches
 41 **league** agreement, proposition
 55 **conjure** appeal earnestly to
 61 **in sunder** apart in pieces
 72 *cassia* cinnamon (a herb)
105 **Charon** Greek god, who conducted the souls of the dead in his boat across the Styx
112 **prattle** speak
118 **mean** poor, humble
131 **silly** feeble, simple

ACT IV

SCENE 1   **Ferdinand, frustrated by the Duchess's fortitude and bent on inducing her despair, endeavours to unsettle her under the guise of reconciliation and gives her a dead man's hand. Bosola reveals to her a tableau of the still figures of her husband and son which she fails to realise are effigies. She wants to die; Ferdinand plans that she should live to suffer torture. Bosola has achieved nearly all the Duke intended for him**

No one can accuse Ferdinand of delicacy. When, in the previous scene, the Duchess asked which prison she was being taken to, Bosola had replied 'To none ... To your palace' (III.5.104). Now she is there Ferdinand asks her gaoler how she is bearing up. 'Nobly ... / ... sad ... / a majesty to adversity' (lines 2–6) is the reply. Bosola finds her tears appealing. With Antonio off the scene there is no one to check his propriety.

Ferdinand assumes she still smoulders like a fire, curses her and leaves. In a prescient gesture, Bosola draws a curtain and informs the revealed Duchess that Ferdinand wants to effect a reconciliation but can only come in darkness as he has vowed never to see her again. She falls in with this stratagem and commands her servants to remove the lights.

Initially, she finds her brother magnanimous. Soon, however, he angers her by referring to her children as bastards. She accuses him of blasphemy; her marriage is a church sacrament. His answer is placatory as he offers her his hand, which she finds strangely cold and then realises, to her horror, that it is not his but a dismembered limb.

Ferdinand leaves as the Duchess calls for light. Bosola draws back another curtain to reveal the figures of her son and Antonio, whose cold hand, he tells her, was his.

She is unaware the figures are waxworks, and curses by pricking pins into a wax image. She would like to freeze to death, in memory of that hand of her supposed dead husband. Or starve; after all 'The Church enjoins fasting' (line 75).

Living becomes a torment for her, because it means she must continually be broken. Webster adds a theatrical image, 'I account this world a tedious theatre, / For I do play a part in't 'gainst my will' (lines 83–4). Increasingly wretched, she wishes even to curse the stars. Bosola points out that her venom is ineffective, that the stars still shine. She warns as she exits, 'you must / Remember, my curse hath a great way to go' (lines 99–100).

Bosola is joined by Ferdinand and, from the pleasure taken planning torture, it can be inferred he witnessed surreptitiously the conversation just past. The Duke confirms that the figures are indeed artificial and Bosola asks him why he has done it. 'To bring her to despair' (line 115) is the bleak response. Bosola shows a rare humanity by protesting that contrition can be achieved less cruelly.

Ferdinand, however, is out to damn her all the way. He will increase the agony by having prostitutes (one of whom he thinks she is) visit her, by uncouth persons serving her meals and, at her breaking point, have the hospitalised mad move nearer her palace. Their deranged noises will certainly disturb her.

Bosola wants to terminate his contract. He stipulates that the secret service he has rendered the Duke absolves him from further contact with the Duchess, unless he is in disguise. Ferdinand agrees his work is nearly done. A last revenge is required. He must murder Antonio in Milan. The Duke's final comment, that doctors grow callous about pain, strangely echoes the Duchess's remark to Antonio when fleeing Ancona, that doctors, once paid, abandon their patients. The Duke obviously feels he has not yet been paid enough, as abandon the Duchess he will not. He will soon learn more, though, about doctors and pain.

> This is a pivotal scene in understanding the Duchess's psyche. She has lost most of the trappings of her status, including her freedom. Since the start she has never had much independence. But now she has reached a point where her very core, spirit and morale, is under threat. Webster plots the transition from a physical to a psychological assault upon her in a number of ways; majesty to adversity, comfort to cruelty, hope to despair, false blessing to full-blown cursing.

> Bosola's attitude to her of superiority has softened to one of admiration. He genuinely thinks Antonio is bad news for her, conflating this with describing her to Ferdinand as noble in her misery. Ferdinand is not prepared to give her so much credit. In her he sees disdain and waywardness where Bosola discerns restraint and passion. But they both have the same aim, to make her forget Antonio. Bosola is again the executor of the plan. He informs the Duchess she can expect a visit from her brother, but in darkness, the implication being that he need not then look upon sin by looking on her. But there is also the hint of a biblical reference, that 'men loved darkness rather than light, because their deeds were evil' (John 3:19).

> Incidentally, it is noteworthy that Bosola refers to Ferdinand as 'Your elder brother' (line 21). In the following scene, Bosola suggests 'she was born first' (IV.2.263). This apparent contradiction is explored elsewhere (see Characterisation – Ferdinand). Bosola's second statement is perhaps made on the evidence of her superior strength of moral standing.

> The Duchess, resigned to her fate, seems unfazed by the prospect of Ferdinand's unseen visit. It is just another horror to be endured. It does not get off to a good start. Ferdinand disparages her

children as animals, albeit playful. He is grudging about their equality in the sight of God despite their insignificance in the eyes of the law.

She challenges this latter notion, key to the play's definition of the relationship between church and state, and epitomised earlier in the roles of the Cardinal and Duke. Indeed, we have seen it combined in one of them, as the Cardinal discards his priestly status to become a soldier; in ecclesiastical dogma, too, giving reluctant validity to the Duchess's marriage 'per verba de presenti' (I.2.392). How dare Ferdinand, therefore, call her children bastards? Marriage is a sacrament, her children are legitimate, and to challenge this is blasphemy.

Ferdinand is impressed with a religious fervour which has, in the past, been somewhat arbitrary. But all this theory deflects him from his purpose, 'To bring her to despair'. And in truth, he has little respect for his sister's (or any) marriage. So he plays his grizzly torture game with the dead man's hand, and when in horror she calls for the lights he slides into the darkness from which he came.

Bosola remains, to carry out Ferdinand's next stage of the Duchess's humiliation. 'The artificial figures' … 'fashion'd out of wax' (lines 55, 63) are real enough to her, all she needs to confirm there is nothing left worth living for.

The image of **dramatic irony**, 'fashion'd out of wax' and stuck with needles contrasts with the falseness of the figures before her. All she sees is lifelessness, the coldness of despair. Bosola disregards Ferdinand's intention, reminding her she is a Christian, that there is hope. But she knows better. She knows she will be lied to even as she dies. So she seizes on an opportunity for martyrdom; she will fast to death.

Bosola tries another tack. Things cannot get any worse. The sting has lost its venom. The bee can be regarded in a friendlier light. What he doesn't say is that a bee that stings can kill and will die.

The Duchess's spirit reasserts itself, assuming a robust response of vitriol. She turns her prayers into curses; cursing life, the stars, the seasons, the world, families and churchmen. She spits 'Remember, my curse hath a great way to go'.

The scene concludes with Bosola reporting 'progress', obviating the need for further torture. Ferdinand, however, has developed a taste for cruelty. A series of tableaux is planned for her; a parade of prostitutes, bawdy and scruffy ruffians, to be capped by a chaotic 'invasion' of madmen. Bosola is losing patience with these bizarre charades. Even the sight of her suffering is too much for him, particularly when he remembers their former working relationship. He is ultimately a servant, and wants to revert to that role. If he must visit her in future, it will be disguised, and 'The business shall be comfort' (line 134). Bosola will soon come to comfort the Duchess, the cold comfort of annihilation. Meanwhile there is Antonio, lurking in Milan, to think about.

80 **wheel** form of torture
118 **furnish** provide
122 **courtesans** prostitutes
139 *agues* illnesses

SCENE 2 The Duchess, fatalistic, retains her equanimity, although surrounded by mad visitors. Bosola, 'tomb-maker', ushers in the executioners, who strangle the Duchess. Her dignity contrasts with Cariola's hysteria. Ferdinand surveys the throttled children, and blames Bosola for not protecting the Duchess. Bosola is appalled at a duke who can offer immunity for a murder he has instigated. The Duchess revives, briefly, and then expires. Bosola resolves to get his revenge in Milan

In the last scene the Duchess calls for lights; in this they go out; for Ferdinand, of sanity, and for the Duchess, of life. 'The robin red-breast and the nightingale / Never live long in cages' (lines 13–14). She enters, with Cariola, to a 'hideous' (line 1) noise, 'the wild consort / Of madmen' (lines 1–2) whose disordered world mirrors Webster's characters; fantasies of witchcraft, lust and corruption. The **irony** is that the Duchess thinks she would go mad with silence, the antithesis of which her brother has planned for driving her to despair. She believes another's **tragedy** blurs the edges of her own. Cariola's opinion is that her mistress looks 'Like to your picture in the gallery, / A deal of life in show, but none in practice' (lines 32–3).

The entrance of 'several sorts of madmen' (line 42) is a variation of the common contemporary 'sport' of visiting the madhouse. This tableau has been brought to her by a deranged brother to 'bring her to despair' (IV.1.115). Perhaps this is an observation by the playwright on the sickness of the middle ranking strata of society from which he himself has come. The range of sickness, too, is characteristic of much the Duke is about to experience.

Into this hell comes Bosola, disguised. He informs the Duchess he is a tomb-maker and she appears to humour him. The reality that he is deadly serious dawns on her with awful potency. He reiterates by ghoulish **metaphors** that she is soon to die. She attempts to assert her authority: 'I am Duchess of Malfi still' (line 139).

His response is artless. 'My trade is to flatter the dead, not the living; / I am a tomb-maker' (lines 144–5). Mock-lightheartedly they discuss the fashions of tombs, and she enquires about the materials from which they are made. He brings in the executioners and she seems fascinated by her 'last presence chamber' (line 168). Cariola cries out for help, at which the Duchess observes only their mad neighbours can hear. As Cariola is led away, the Duchess commends the children to her care.

The Duchess is matter-of-fact about her death, enquiring how she will die and forgiving her executioners for speeding up the natural process. She sends a message to her brothers thanking them for this gift of death; hoping now, like vultures, 'They then may feed in quiet' (line 233). She will indulge in prevarication no more. She instructs her executioners to pull hard, kneeling because heaven only admits those on their knees.

Bosola orders the children be strangled too, and that Cariola be brought in. She sees her mistress 'sleep', the **irony** being that the Duchess is, still, only unconscious. Cariola pleads that she is not ready to die (compare this with line 199, 'I will die with her') and fights for her life; announcing that she is to be married, that she is a spy, and biting and scratching her killers as they throttle her and drag her body out.

Ferdinand enters. Bosola shows him the bodies of the children, which fails to move him. The Duke then turns to look at his dazzling twin, whose face he had been unable to look upon. Ferdinand suppresses his regrets by accusing Bosola of not protecting the Duchess better, 'thou has done much ill, well' (line 285).

Bosola, outraged by the Duke's offer of magnanimous pardon, demands his pay and is summarily dismissed 'into some unknown part o'th' world' (line 320). Bosola curses for being duped into such loathsome evil. It was for love of them he did it, revealing a vital truth about his inner nature, that he 'rather sought / To appear a true servant than an honest man' (lines 326–7).

Ferdinand exits, finally showing a mad remorse. Bosola realises a peaceable conscience is worth more than money and wonders yet, as the Duchess seems warm to his touch, if it is too late. She calls for Antonio. Bosola assures her that her husband is alive and reconciled to her brothers. Her death cannot long be deferred which makes its inevitability a more poignant **tragedy**. The possibility of a happy outcome, however remote, makes good drama.

She dies with 'mercy' on her lips and Bosola is left alone with his lie, weeping, not from fear, but pity. He picks up her body 'to the reverend dispose / Of some good women' (lines 365–6). He will have his revenge in Milan.

> The Duchess is startled by noise, hideous yet consoling. Ferdinand had hinted earlier these people might not be mad, but a theatrical masque, 'I will send her masques ... If she can sleep the better for it' (IV.1.122, 129). The Duchess may be deceived, but this is theatre and these are actors playing mad people. So our complicity is well founded.

> Cariola believes they must be at the bottom of their luck. Foolish talk, retorts the Duchess. Last time she called her a 'superstitious fool' (III.2.317), although then Cariola had been right. This time, sadly, it is going to be the mistress who is right.

> Once again we glimpse Webster's political acumen, demonstrating his Protestant sympathies. As well as vilifying superstition he questions what sort of a Pope can it be who is cheered out of depressive illness with the sport of madmen?

Bosola enters in disguise. 'Is he mad too?' (line 114) asks the Duchess. He does not disguise, however, the task he has in hand, that of being a tomb-maker. The Duchess seeks assurance that he knows who she is, even if she doesn't know who he is. Has he got the right person? 'Am I not thy Duchess?' (line 132). He leads her by degrees to accept her fate with the crude **imagery** of the grave, 'Thou art a box of worm seed' (line 123). His description of 'a lark in a cage' (line 128) is reminiscent of hers earlier of robins and nightingales who 'Never live long in cages' (line 14).

The Duchess began to think of death early in the play, appropriating **metaphors** like 'shroud' (I.2.415) to veil her prescience. Even under house-arrest the inevitable procession towards annihilation has been delayed by tortures organised by a deranged brother and delivered by a servant apparently devoid of conscience. Bosola, this absolute servant, is again central in her final act, and his words of remorse seem a little late, 'I am angry with myself ... I loath'd the evil, yet I lov'd / You that did counsel it' (lines 319, 325–6).

Bosola has doubled as bellman and coffin-man. He sings a song reminiscent of the madmen. As matters deteriorate, Cariola accurately assesses that they are in the presence of 'villains, tyrants, murderers' (line 193) to which only the mad can respond. Bosola finds the maid tiresome and demands her removal as 'noise' (line 196).

The Duchess's calm contrasts with her maid's hysteria. She is given an opportunity to 'Say her prayers, ere she sleep' (line 202). Her instinct is that such an exercise has not only not been very effective up to now but is the sort of superstitious activity which will distract her from composure; an activity best recommended for children.

She then asks and is answered by the three most chilling words of the play: 'What death?', 'Strangling' (line 203). Neither death nor its manner affect her. She sees it as a gift and kneels to heaven, not her brothers, cannibals or vultures who on her death, 'may feed in quiet' (line 233).

Bosola turns to dealing with the 'noise' and the noise's less noisy charges. His clinical efficiency is horribly admirable. He has been delicate with the Duchess. Dispatching the rest is accompanied by his dark humour. 'You kept her counsel', he says to Cariola, referring to the intimacy which subsists between mistress and maid, 'now you shall keep ours' (line 242). By silencing.

Ferdinand tiptoes in to find his task done. Bosola's confirmation is accusatory, 'murther shrieks out' (line 256), 'the screech-owl' of his recent song to the Duchess. Ferdinand responds with the first glimmerings of remorse, 'She and I were twins' (line 261). I have murdered half of myself, a psychological suicide.

Bosola is unimpressed. Relatives are always at enmity with each other, says this man without family. Ferdinand begs, 'Let me see her face again' (line 266). Let me turn the clock back. Let me undo what I have done. I did it in an unbalanced state of jealousy. You should have stopped me.

Ferdinand knows his sister was innocent. He has been too busy exacting revenge to recognise that before. Revenge, the enemy of balance, clouds judgement. That is why, as the law developed, revenge was abandoned as a legal route to retribution. Ferdinand paints revenge as vindictive. Bosola should have taken the Duchess to sanctuary, or bravely protected her by his sword. Finally, the Duke fools himself it was his sister's marriage, in depriving him of a mass of wealth, that was the main cause of her death. His quick recovery from self-recrimination is signalled by an **oxymoron**, 'justice is perverted quite' (line 300), coming from a cynical Bosola who decides that if he is to be blamed he will also be paid.

Ferdinand is no more able to withstand this kind of confrontation from Bosola than he was from his sister. He wills Bosola to 'Never look upon me more' (line 311). Before, he would not look on the Duchess. The reason for both evasions is the same. Her's and then Bosola's perceptions are far too searching for comfort.

It is now Bosola's turn to accuse. Ferdinand, on his way out to madness, subtly changes his injunction of banishment of Bosola. 'Never look upon' becomes 'That I may never see thee' (line 321), an admission that Bosola has won the war of nerves and cannot be persuaded to look away. So Ferdinand himself must avert his gaze.

Bosola feigns hurt at his rejection. Faithful to the point of recklessness, he claims to hate the evil he has had to perform.

Ferdinand has tried to launch out on a final speech more than once. Each time he does, he is frustrated by a more articulate Bosola. At last he does go off into the darkness of an animal world, his increasingly natural habitat.

Bosola stays on. He has lost all peace of mind. He has little wealth, apart from that which he stole from the Duchess. He has been hired servant to brothers whose conscious policy appears to have been not to pay him. The Duchess briefly revives, but the life Bosola has stolen from her seems to be slipping away. Again, lies are easier expressed than truth, half lies easier than whole lies. As she dies she whispers the word he longs to appropriate; 'Mercy' (line 347).

Bosola now really is alone. He launches into another of the play's great speeches. Bending over his dead Duchess, he repeats Ferdinand's affirmation of her innocence, her sleep of peace compared with his troubled consciousness. His pity now has gone beyond his fear. Why had he not shown penitence whilst she was still alive?

From being frozen, asleep, he is now awake, and hot with shame. He will carry her body to those worthier than he. The cruel tyrant will surely not deny that. Who is that tyrant? Ferdinand? His own conscience? He picks her up as a lover. He is a lover, but only because she is dead. Because he is decadent he can only love the dead and the decaying.

8 **discourse to** discuss with
12 **durance** endurance, imprisonment
34 **reverend** respected
36 **Fortune** Greek goddess of plenty, whose gifts may be good or bad, often visually represented as blindfolded, whose votives entreated her to hide their bodily defects from their husbands

70 **quire** choir

84 **allum** astringent chemical, cure for constipation

105 **caroche** coach

110 **milch** milk

162 **charnel** vault or cemetery

205 **apoplexy** fit

252 **traverse** curtain

256 **murther** murder

286 **quicken** sharpen

350 **turtles' feathers** soft bedding of dove down

ACT V

SCENE 1   In Milan, Antonio reviews his chances of reconciliation with the Aragon brothers. They have seized his land and passed it on to nonentities. Delio supports a decision to make one final gesture to the Cardinal

Antonio and Delio arrive in Milan ahead of Bosola. Antonio, ignorant of his wife's death, hopes yet for a reconciliation with her brothers. Delio is more realistic. The Duke and the Cardinal have confiscated their brother-in-law's property and enticed him into their trap. 'I cannot think they mean well to your life, / That do deprive you of your means of life' (lines 11–12).

The new 'inheritor' of Antonio's lands, the Marquis of Pescara, enters and Delio asks Pescara for a citadel within Antonio's former estates. Pescara refuses.

Julia enters, carrying a letter from the Cardinal to Pescara requesting him to make this same citadel over to her. Pescara immediately acquiesces. Delio simulates affront at this preference which Pescara excuses by saying that the land was stolen from Antonio and therefore could hardly be given to anyone else with justice or a good conscience; ''tis a gratification / Only due to a strumpet' (lines 45–6), and adds 'Learn, good Delio, / To ask noble things of me, and you shall find / I'll be a noble giver' (lines 52–4). The message to Antonio is brutal; if the Cardinal had his brother-in-law's best interests at heart he would hardly be passing his forfeited lands to a mistress.

Pescara leaves, announcing that Ferdinand has arrived in Milan, sick. The **dramatic irony** is that the Duke now suffers from a madness he tried to inflict on the Duchess.

Antonio decides it is time for some action. He has access to the Cardinal's bedroom which he will visit by night. By pressure and cajoling he hopes to effect a reconciliation, or at least bring matters to a head. Delio promises to support him and they swear friendship in adversity.

Act V is the Act of the Aftermath! The dramatist wants us to look beyond the end to what happens when good is gone. This final **dénouement** has always been a critical perplexity of the play. Killing off the **protagonist** so early presents the playwright with an intriguing problem; to command audience interest when the hero is only a memory.

Antonio may have been a good counsellor, but he has proved a flawed husband. His reactions under pressure are suspect. The friends he makes are shallow and unwholesome. This is the man our heroine has chosen with such abandon. (Or did she chose him out of a lusty desperation, worried she might otherwise embark on a life of permanent widowhood?) Delio cannot understand what sort of a man can still be optimistic about in-laws who demand his head and his heart, not necessarily intact. There have been some aspects of Antonio and Delio to admire. But how will they behave under moral pressure now the moral beacon is extinguished?

Pescara is worthy, but uncomfortable 'inheriting' Antonio's confiscated lands. He refuses Delio's request not because Julia wants it but because the citadel has come to him falsely. He would not want a friend to come by such a tainted thing. He would not want a friend to be put at risk with a property, ownership of which might be questioned in a future when the regime changes.

Julia wants it. And Julia is used to getting what she wants. Let her use it for her lust, implies Pescara. Let her use this stolen thing as a brothel. Pescara says to Delio 'I'll be a noble giver'; this property is not a noble gift. He leaves to care for his sick acquaintance.

A man who can possibly imagine that a meaningful relationship can result from the sort of fright Antonio intends to try and force the

Cardinal into a reconciliation must be naive. Indeed, Antonio never has had a worthwhile bond with the callous Cardinal. Perhaps that is why such an ingenuous counsellor can have Delio as his 'lov'd and best friend' (line 76).

2 **misdoubt** doubt

9 **suit** pursuit, request

13 **an heretic** of disbelieving opinion

14 **shape** accommodate

20 **demenses** domains, land

46 **strumpet** prostitute

SCENE 2   **The court sympathises with a demented Ferdinand. He suffers another uncontrollable attack. The stage clears to leave the Cardinal in discussion with Bosola. Julia calls them to supper and expresses her lust for Bosola, who is busy plotting with the Cardinal how to kill Antonio. Later, Julia, finding Bosola alone, begins to woo. He tests her love with a task, to discover why the Cardinal is so distracted. After hiding Bosola she probes the Cardinal who resists with dire warnings but then relents, confiding he has been responsible for his sister's murder. He poisons Julia, after she has confessed she cannot keep his secret because Bosola is hidden in the room. Bosola emerges, and he and the Cardinal continue planning Antonio's demise. Alone, Bosola soliloquises how he will save Antonio**

Pescara confronts the doctor as to when a visit to Ferdinand may be appropriate. The doctor diagnoses lycanthropia which Pescara candidly admits he'll need a dictionary to define! The doctor explains that it is an illness in which the patient behaves like a wolf, digging up bodies. Ferdinand has been found howling in the churchyard, shouldering a man's dismembered limb.

The doctor and Pescara are joined by the two Aragon brothers and Malateste, with Bosola lurking. Ferdinand begins another episode, attacking his shadow. Perhaps he thinks it is his sister stalking him; he says he will throttle it, much as he had done her.

The Duke tries to take his clothes off but is nervous of the doctor's reaction, 'Hide me from him. Physicians are like kings, / They brook no contradiction' (lines 64–5).

The doctor prescribes a pickling juice. He has had enough nonsense from his patient and earlier had promised stronger treatment in the event of a relapse. He delivers a buffeting. The **pun** on 'caper' is not lost on Ferdinand and he starts to leap about, nearly flattening the flattering doctor. The patient is eventually subdued, the doctor ruefully admitting that his treatment, meeting madness with madness, hasn't worked.

The Cardinal attempts to gloss over his brother's poor behaviour by recounting an old family myth, of decay and murder, the misappropriation of wealth and a cry for justice. The **dramatic irony** is that these are the themes of the play.

The stage clears except for Bosola and the Cardinal, who cloaks his knowledge of his sister's destiny. Their scheming is interrupted by Julia announcing supper. The Cardinal brusquely declines. In an **aside** she confides her lust for Bosola, and leaves. The Cardinal hurries to ask a favour: kill Antonio. That will free the Duchess to make a better match. Bosola asks how to execute. Follow Delio, the Cardinal replies. He's Antonio's friend.

Bosola, left alone, doubts the Cardinal is ignorant of the Duchess's death. He will employ a similar cunning, 'There cannot be a surer way to trace, / Than that of an old fox' (lines 147–8).

Wild-eyed Julia joins him, phallicly waving a pistol, teasing by **innuendo** and enquiring who he bribed to feed her a love potion which has made her desire him insatiably since she saw him at Amalfi, and how she must have her longing assuaged immediately. They embrace and Bosola disarms her. She finds his wooing lacking in finesse but delights in a bit of soldierly rough.

Bosola is not concentrating on Julia's 'courtship', but on how this new liaison can be put to good use. Julia assures him she is impetuous, inviting him to ask her a special favour. She little expects this dogged servant's response to be so swift. He asks her to find out why the Cardinal is melancholic. If it is because the Cardinal's reputation with the Emperor is on the wane 'like the mice / That forsake falling houses, I would shift / To other dependence' (lines 203–5). This gives her the chance to invite him to become her banker, an invitation she herself received from Delio in Act II. He prevaricates, pressing his commission to 'intelligence' (line 213). She agrees 'Cunningly'; another of Webster's **ironies** as she is singularly lacking in cunning; likely, too, another of his sexual **puns**.

She promises instant satisfaction and he hides. The Cardinal returns, banning all visitors from his brother. In an **aside** he fears Ferdinand, 'may reveal the murther' (line 224). He muses he would be rid of his mistress. She greets him, pressing him to tell her why he is so discountenanced, a confidence he resists, knowing she is not skilled at keeping secrets. She will have it from him; he has after all kept her big secret of adultery. She wants to be put to the same kind of test. She will regret it, he says, but finally relents. Four days ago by his authority his sister and her children were strangled. Julia's horror is as he anticipated. She retorts he will be his own undoing; she cannot conceal such a thing. Unless, he replies, you swear silence by the Bible, which she says she will kiss 'Most religiously' (line 272). And silence it is because, in an act of blasphemy, he fulfils his prophecy of her ruin, poisons the book and she kisses the poison.

Bosola emerges too late from his 'secret' place. Julia reflects on how justice is being done. The Cardinal's secret is already known to 'that fellow; / He overheard it; that was the cause I said / It lay not in me to conceal it' (lines 279–81). Bosola chides her for not poisoning the Cardinal. She admits to weakness and dies. Bosola is quick to distract and demand payment for past services, not this time from a mad Duke but from 'a great man, like yourself' (line 285). Met by Bosola's calmness in the face of such calumny, the Cardinal tempers his violence with cunning, once more with offers of honours to come. He still wants Bosola's confirmation that he will carry out Antonio's murder. That assured, with a resurgence of arrogance, he orders Bosola to carry the dead Julia from the room. Bosola is comfortable to be back in grumbling servant mode again.

Whether by cunning to implicate, or anxiety to ensure success by an excess of power, the Cardinal attempts to persuade Bosola to accept a small army to carry out his last commission. Bosola knows to act alone. They make plans to meet when all is done. Bosola, too, has a key to the Cardinal's bedchamber.

Alone, Bosola pities Antonio. He will seek him out, not to kill but to protect from these ruthless 'cruel biters' (line 336). He will seek to join him 'With the sword of justice' (line 340). There is **dramatic irony** in Bosola calling down justice; that such a man can still be capable of such worthy thoughts. His haunted vision of the Duchess is now being replaced by penitence, perhaps even restitution, 'That throws men down, only to raise them up' (line 343).

Ferdinand is an uncooperative patient. At times he acts like a wolf, digging up dead bodies, most recently a human limb. Was the dead man's hand he held out to his sister an early indication of his lycanthropia? Is his sister's recent death a spur to his frequenting graveyards?

His wolf obsession is not new. In Act IV Scene 2 he reproaches Bosola for the Duchess's murder and predicts that 'The wolf shall find her grave, and scrape it up; / Not to devour the corpse, but to discover / The horrid murther' (lines 303–5).

Ferdinand combines mania with sharp insight. He is the centre of attention and his language indicates mood swings; attempting to throttle his shadow, studying the art of patience, reacting paranoically to his doctor, and insulting aggression just as applicable to himself as his victims.

The Cardinal seems to be on edge, the first time he has been present and not held centre-stage. Ferdinand's deranged behaviour has obliterated his former deference and the Cardinal finds this new confrontation a threat. His anxiety is compounded by Bosola and Pescara's curiosity. So he obfuscates behind a myth about a family ghost, a woman murdered by relatives. This **dramatic irony** is very close to home. It was the Cardinal who counselled his sister's death; Ferdinand and Bosola who were the executioners.

It would not be worthy of Webster's economical use of characters to introduce Julia in one scene and then lose track of her. She slides in in a most appealing light. She has found it difficult to decide which man to go for; a cardinal for comfort or a spy for spice. The Cardinal is going to seed, but is powerful and rich; Bosola is poor but has kept his physical trim, 'What an excellent shape hath that fellow' (line 120). Finding Bosola alone, she lets him know her lust for him. She views a change of sexual allegiance as physically exciting and readily agrees to prove her longing by a favour, adding a brazen offer. It isn't her style to hint; she is well enough set up to be his provider.

Bosola's mind is on his next assignment and he will not be distracted. Once more the arras proves an excellent piece of furniture for hiding behind. In Act I Cariola hid whilst the Duchess wooed. Now Bosola hides whilst Julia woos him by remote.

The Cardinal is tired of dallying with her, and barely conceals it. He tries to deflect Julia's curiosity about his current melancholy by a paradox, 'The only way to make thee keep my counsel / Is not to tell thee' (lines 238–9).

Counsel has ended up a mockery. Advice is by definition a gentle confidence, remaining often an unknown secret. But evasiveness obstructs Julia's purpose and she will have none of it. Throughout her relationship with the Cardinal she has maintained discretion in their adultery. She is as tired of that concealment as he is of her. So, although he warns her that knowledge is danger, she drags from him his guilty secret.

Immediately she regrets what she has done and he misinterprets her regret as betrayal. He has already betrayed his guilt to Bosola. He now betrays his religious status by poisoning a Bible he insists she kiss. Murdering her combines a blasphemy with an act of atheism.

Bosola realises what is happening too late. The Cardinal's question to him 'Wherefore com'st thou hither?' follows strangely after Julia's last words 'I go, / I know not whither' (line 284). Is Bosola come from where Julia has gone, hardly likely to be heaven?

Bosola's response is banal. He has come for his reward. The Cardinal's reaction is much like his brother's, passionate anger. The Cardinal is dismayed that here is another dangerous witness, one unafraid to blackmail.

These two men who lack compassion or honour must negotiate each others' complicity. To kill Antonio is the next commission.

After, that is, Bosola has carried another woman's body out – the first his mistress past, the second a mistress not now ever to be.

Bosola mutters dispassionately, 'Believe me, you have done a very happy turn' (line 321). Was Bosola only using Julia to aid his intelligencing, after which he would have had to do something to her like the Cardinal has just done so conveniently for him? Or is he slipping into a fait accompli with superb malleability?

Bosola knows there is danger everywhere. The Cardinal will not rest until this dangerous witness is silenced. Bosola will seek out Antonio, not to kill but to try and make amends by ensuring his safety. We know Bosola is sincere because he confides it in **soliloquy**.

25 **Paracelsus** Bombastus Paracelsus, a recently famous Swiss physician who dabbled in magic. Webster is unlikely to have missed the **pun** intrinsic in his first name and appropriate to the present setting, particularly in mind of views severally expressed throughout the play about the fallibility of the medical profession

60 **salamander** lizard, the skin of which was supposed to be able to resist fire. Ferdinand has just been talking about going to hell, so the doctor's suggestion is perhaps not so far fetched after all

62 **cocatrice** or cockatrix; a mythical cock with a serpent's tail

71 **peril** risk

75 **cullis** a nourishing meat broth

76 **Barber-Chirurgeon's** doctor/surgeons

124 **style** set up for

136 **Jews** Antonio has a reputation for embezzlement and the embattled Jewish community, denied citizenship and frequently unfairly pilloried by reputation, are fair game to contemporary playwrights for vilification

143 **basilisks** salamanders

173 **fair** beautiful

181 **familiar** intimate

188 **purloins** obtains

198 **wondrous** unexpectedly

214 **cabinet** cupboard, closet

225 **consumption** decay, weariness

243 **rack** one of the methods used to extract confession was torture by rack, a frame onto which the body was strapped and then rotated, often over a fire

257 **adamant** hard (as diamond)

267 **how settles this** how is this matter to be settled

329 **frost-nail'd** nail-imprinted boots in icy weather

SCENE 3   **Antonio and Delio are near the Cardinal's lodging.**
Antonio hears an echo of their conversation which sounds
like the ghostly voice of his wife. He must determine his
fate once and for all, for good or bad

Delio and Antonio are outside the Cardinal's window, near the ruins of
an ancient abbey by the camp fortifications. Delio tells Antonio that the
cloister 'Gives the best echo that you ever heard; / So hollow, and so
dismal, and withal / So plain in the distinction of our words, / That many
have suppos'd it is a spirit / That answers' (lines 5–9). Antonio pompously
expounds the import of history but proceeds to the prosaic, 'all things
have their end' (line 17); Webster's hint that the play is nearly over.

An echo picks up their conversation. Delio has his opinion
confirmed but Antonio supposes he hears the dismal tones of the
Duchess, 'a face folded in sorrow' (line 44) which confirms his fear that
he may 'never see her more' (line 41). Delio believes Antonio should heed
the stonewall echo's admonition to 'fly your fate' (line 35).

They know that death may meet them along the labyrinths but the
experience stiffens Antonio's resolve to attempt a last reconciliation with
the Cardinal. 'Necessity compels me' (line 32) to 'Lose all, or nothing'
(line 49).

This scene and the next provide a much-needed lull in the pace
of the play. Delio is the realist. The echo is caused by the simple
configuration of the buildings. (Ruined abbeys, post Henry VIII,
are an English not an Italian phenomenon.)

Antonio is superstitious. He thinks churches have a propensity
for human experience. His supernatural acuity leads him to
discern his wife's morbid voice. The **irony** is that he is ignorant of
his wife's death or that her grave is situated near the echo's source.
He comforts himself that, being night, she and the children are in
bed. Webster cannot resist a playful twist; two of the echoes are not
exact replicas of Antonio's original. His 'my wife's voice' becomes
'Ay, wife's voice' (line 26), his 'To fly your fate' becomes 'O fly your

fate' (line 35). The dramatist is mocking religious superstition again.

'Never see her more' is Antonio's stimulus to act. 'For better fall once, than be ever falling' (V.1.73) was worthy enough theory, but two scenes ago. Now he is resolute, 'I will not henceforth save myself by halves' (line 48).

1 **Yond's** beyond is

6 **withal** altogether, in addition, as well

13 **injuries** battering

44 **folded in** overtaken by

45 **fancy** imagination, delusion

   ague indisposition

SCENE 4   **The Cardinal ensures that, by dire threats and solemn promises, he will not be disturbed disposing of Julia's body and killing Bosola, who overhears the murderous intention towards him. In the night-time confusion Bosola accidentally stabs Antonio, and has a servant carry the body towards the Cardinal's room**

The Cardinal **soliloquises** how he will conceal his grizzly work removing Julia's body involving Bosola who, the task complete, will be killed too. Bosola, overhearing, enters, followed by Ferdinand, whose loud ravings contrast his murmured 'Strangling is a very quiet death' (line 33). The Duke leaves and Antonio, led by a servant, enters the darkened room. In a reverie about 'taking' the Cardinal at his prayers, he is stabbed from behind by Bosola who mistakes him for the Cardinal and cries out 'I'll not give thee so much leisure as to pray' (line 45).

A light reveals the mistake, and Bosola wills Antonio to a mercifully quick end. Antonio ponders the superficiality of pleasure, commends himself to Delio, expresses a wish for his son to avoid court life, and dies. Bosola arranges for the body to be carried to the Cardinal.

The scene is played out in subdued light, enhancing a sense of shifting reality and isolation. The Cardinal schemes for his brother to be alone in order to provide cover for Bosola's removal of Julia's body. What the Cardinal in fact achieves is a fatal isolation of himself and this stirs a moribund conscience. Bosola knows, Bosola must die.

The **soliloquy**'s convention is corrupted (and the Cardinal's sincerity is questioned) by having Bosola overhear. Webster has undermined our certainties before. And one brother's soliloquy is followed by the other's **solipsism**. Ferdinand shuffles on, muttering that strangling is a quiet way to kill. He is still in the past, still conspiring his sister's death. His analysis was right and wrong: his sister's death was very quiet; Cariola's was not.

Antonio surmises that if he surprises the Cardinal 'At his prayers, there were hope of pardon' (line 43). This is not the avenging Hamlet who will not kill Claudius at prayer in case the royal soul is saved. Antonio wants the Cardinal to be softened to reconciliation by prayer.

Bosola knows his 'death is plotted' (line 38). He will have to be cautious. In the confusion of darkness Bosola mistakes Antonio for the Cardinal and kills him. That is the usual interpretation of Bosola's 'mistake'.

But Webster may have meant something different. There is a perfectly possible and radical alternative, which is that Bosola has achieved his final and intended commission at last. Let us recite the facts:

- Bosola has quite sufficient reason to continue to fear Antonio, who is bound to find out eventually who killed his wife. They have always been rivals; over horsemanship, service and as counsellors.
- Bosola knows Antonio well; certainly his looks, the way he moves, his voice. It is admittedly dark, but Antonio's talking to his servant is sufficiently loud for Bosola to hear the phrase 'At his prayers' and quote it to his victim as he kills.
- It is the servant, not Bosola, who calls Antonio's death a misfortune. Indeed, Bosola orders the servant to 'Smother thy pity' (line 51).
- Bosola wants Antonio to die quickly, presumably before there can be any further betrayals of confidence. He therefore divulges his

news concerning the Duchess to Antonio, knowing how distressing this will be, and then brutally demands 'Break, heart' (line 70).

• Bosola tells the servant, who 'seem'st to have lov'd Antonio' (line 72), to take the body to the Cardinal who commissioned the execution. In Act V Scene 2 Bosola's sincerity is beyond doubt because it was a **soliloquy**. He did not intend to kill Antonio, at least at that moment. Now the mistake has happened, however, Bosola may not be too unhappy. He must imagine that he is bound to be paid a reward at last.

• Bosola's parenthetic remark '(O direful misprision!)' (line 79), an acknowledgement of his 'mistake', may well refer to the fact that he had intended to kill the Cardinal first, and that he has therefore still that last task to undertake.

• It would not be out of character for Bosola to admit to this mistake to confuse a servant he now knows he needs to kill but must choose with care the moment to do so. Meanwhile, he is a useful 'common bier for churchyards' (V.2.307).

3 **suffer** allow
10 **sensibly** reasonably
19 **osier** willow
39 **desert** what we deserve
41 **confident** sure, bold
58 **kindle** revive
64 **wanton** indisciplined, uncontrolled
67 **ague** illness, disease
68 **vexation** trouble, disturbance, irritation

SCENE 5   Bosola, with Antonio's body, arrives at the Cardinal's
           lodging and pronounces the Cardinal's imminent
           demise. The Cardinal cries for help. His courtiers ignore
           him, anticipating this to be a test. To ensure the
           Cardinal's door remains locked Bosola kills the servant
           and wounds the Cardinal but is caught off guard by
           Ferdinand, who enters and, in delusion and for good
           measure, stabs them both. Bosola kills both Duke and
           Cardinal. Courtiers burst in and Bosola brings them up
           to date before dying himself. Delio enters with Antonio's
           son as heir

The Cardinal wanders on with troubled conscience, reading a religious
book. Bosola follows as the Cardinal expects, but not to carry out Julia's
body but to carry in Antonio's.

   Bosola immediately proclaims the Cardinal is next. The Cardinal
cries for help, just as Cariola urged the Duchess to do in Act IV. Then
the only ones to hear were the Amalfi mad, now it is the Milan courtiers.
The Cardinal, stalling for time, offers to share his wealth with Bosola
who, from previous experience, regards this to be a hollow promise. The
courtiers hear the Cardinal's cry but, remembering their honour, refrain
from interference. Pescara decides to investigate and the others follow to
watch. Bosola is taking no chances with the servant and deals him a
death-blow.

   The Cardinal, pleading for his own life, notices the body of
Antonio, whose death, Bosola explains, was an accident. He also explains
to the Cardinal that, by killing his sister, he unbalanced the scales of
justice, leaving no redress but that of violence. Ignoring appeals for
mercy, Bosola stabs the Cardinal. His brother's yelps for help bring on
Ferdinand lost in a fantasy of some glorious battlefield. With **dramatic
irony** he mistakes his brother for a devil and wounds him further, also
fatally striking at Bosola.

   Bosola summons up final strength to sink his sword in Ferdinand,
the main cause of his undoing. The courtiers burst in. Bosola explains
that what they see is a result of bloody revenge for a trio of crimes; the
murder of the Duchess, the poisoning of Julia and, despite his part as
'main actor' in all of it, the neglect of himself.

Bosola admits he cannot tell exactly how Antonio comes to be dead. But, he says with Webster's **satire**, it must have been the sort of mistake often experienced in the theatre. The impact of his last couplet, 'Let worthy minds ne'er stagger in distrust / To suffer death or shame for what is just' (lines 102–3), is clouded as he dissociates himself from those worthy minds by a final phrase, 'Mine is another voyage' (line 104).

The courtiers, with death all around them, are lost without a leader and turn their thoughts to an heir. Delio enters with Antonio's son and, touching on the fragile nature of fame, directs that they all should proclaim the boy's succession at once.

> This claustrophobic **tragedy** closes by the opening up again of promise. But in the euphoria of Delio's grandiloquence the Duchess's only son by her first marriage, and her real successor, appears to have been strangely forgotten!

> An empty stage is symbol of an exhausted story. The Cardinal enters, reading, a stage device to indicate depressed melancholia. Not any book does he read, at that, but a religious text, confirmation of an awakened conscience and Webster's **irony**; a criminal Cardinal studying the theology of hell.

> Bosola enters and signals immediately that he has come to kill again. Bribes and calls for help are too late. All Bosola allows is the Cardinal's retreat to where dead Julia lies, a deeper seclusion where shouting for help to his agitated courtiers becomes more difficult.

> The servant has done his job, and is unceremoniously killed. It is perhaps this murder more than any other, the ruthless removal of a defenceless and anonymous underling, that demonstrates the extent to which Bosola's dehumanising has gone, casting doubt on the genuineness of any expression of contrition.

> Bosola urges the Cardinal to pray, a wry reversal of professional roles. Bosola must keep his purpose sharp, his angst fired but controlled for ultimate revenge. He does not make a clean kill of the Cardinal; his expertise at butchery has been plentifully practised. But he is an experienced torturer too and prolongs this death to madden his victim.

Bosola, in turn, is confronted by the torturer-in-chief. Ferdinand sees three bodies on the floor and thinks he is on a battlefield, which in a sense he is. Here is a chance for frenzied revenge on a brother who has always patronised him, and recently kept him locked up without even the consolation of friends; a chance too, to get even with a too-clever servant.

So both the Cardinal and Bosola receive their final pay from Ferdinand, who delivers death blows with manic logic. As he himself dies by the hand of the wounded Bosola he once more locates truth, if somewhat haphazardly; and there will not be a person in the theatre who will argue with his cry 'My sister, oh! my sister, there's the cause on't' (line 70).

Bosola, dying too, has only contempt for the Cardinal, 'I do glory / That thou, which stood'st like a huge pyramid / ... / Shalt end in a little point, a kind of nothing' (lines 75–8). Just the oblivion the Cardinal craves. Except that Webster graces the Cardinal with a last **irony**; because, whatever the pyramid's dimensions are, it stands remembered still when Webster writes more than four thousand years on, a wonder of the ancient world.

The courtiers break into the carnage too late. Bosola tells them every death is because of revenge. That he, a man of good nature, has been 'Neglected' (line 86). That Antonio has been killed by the kind of 'mistake as I have often seen / In a play' (lines 94–5), a mistake attributed by Bosola to the playwright who writes his lines in a dramatic whimsy gone wrong, not undertaken by Bosola's freewill, but as an act of predestination, in much the same way Judas Iscariot is depicted in the Bible fulfilling prophecy by betraying Jesus. The inevitability of evil is a part of divine planning, a sacred dogma of Puritanism, and Webster's own **ironic** commentary on Bosola's displacement of responsibility. It was meant to be, he implies.

There has been a dark inevitability about Bosola's fate. At the start he sets out with one objective – to extract 'payment' for past slights and services. Soon he realises that getting money out of the Aragon brothers is like getting blood out of stones. So he gets blood out of them instead. By the end he has achieved what he set out to do and meets death with equanimity. His mission has been contracted by an amoral determinism to an evil mischief, with the malice of revenge as its driving force.

Webster allows neither the just nor the unjust to survive. But the morally neutral slip by. Of the courtiers, Delio finds his place midway between the good and the neutral. He leads the future onto the stage, too late to fulfil his promise to Antonio at their final parting to 'beget / The more compassion' (V.3.52–3.) but in time to help the boy to inherit 'In's mother's right' (line 112).

Has Webster been accurate? Of the Duchess's five children it is the son of her first marriage who should now inherit the Dukedom of Malfi. This inheritance was implicitly acknowledged by Ferdinand at the time of the Duchess's banishment from Ancona with his instruction to the Cardinal to 'Write to the Duke of Malfi, my young nephew / She had by her first husband' (III.3.68–9). Yet here is Delio with an apparently false heir. We do well to pay close attention to the words Webster gives Delio, 'In's mother's right'. No more and no less: Whatever the Duchess's right's are, they are not the Dukedom of Malfi, of which she was only dowager or caretaker until her son could inherit legally at adulthood. Webster is a fastidious lawyer and he is unlikely to have made an inadvertent error. It is more likely that we are witnesses again of his irresistible playfulness, a last critique of this court's corruption. Or perhaps, in a play so full of warped judgements the final injustice is the wrong son inheriting.

The play is done and the major characters are dead, the good with the bad. The stuff of **tragedy** is that noble integrity only achieves its end in the fate of death.

16 **raise** summon

17 **confin'd** restricted

29 **jest** joke, fun

31 **ope** open

51 **adverse party** other side

60 **barber** in Webster's day barbers performed the role of dentists

PART THREE

CRITICAL APPROACHES

One of the devices that Webster employs in his writing which makes his work so compelling is the paradox that he is simply not interested in simplification. We discover, time and again when studying *The Duchess of Malfi*, that we are led into what appears to be a settled opinion about a theme or character, and then quite quickly we have to revise that impression. Whether he does this because of the perversity of his own personality, or out of a certain playfulness, or because of his lawyer's training which strives always to see both points of view, it may be difficult (and pointless) to discern. Suffice it to say that it is a characteristic of Webster's style that he leads us into certain perspectives only to unsettle any judgements reached upon them.

RECURRING THEMES

REVENGE

Too often *The Duchess of Malfi* is glibly categorised as a 'revenge **tragedy**' with little attempt to expand or challenge the definition or examine other pressing claims to a dominance of theme. Nevertheless as a **Renaissance genre** revenge demands attention.

Prior to the Renaissance revenge was a common way in which justice brought balance to wrong-doing, particularly murder. One of the benefits of the enlightenment for which the Renaissance is justly renowned is the development of a state legal system which became progressively more sophisticated as courts of law became more established.

By the time Webster was writing, personal revenge was generally not only unlawful but an indicator of a malaise in a society infected by anarchy. Nevertheless revenge drama was popular because it gave ordinary people an opportunity through theatre and the imagination to redress wrongs ignored by the courts. But the audience's view would be an ambivalent mix of sympathy for the wronged individual and a moralistic antipathy towards the avengers for taking the law into their own hands. The tension was often resolved in the theatre by the revenger achieving satisfaction, but then themselves becoming the victim of a further act of revenge.

In *The Duchess of Malfi* the patterns of revenge often cross each other. The Aragon brothers (and don't miss Webster's possible **pun** on Aragon!), the Duke Ferdinand and the Cardinal, move early in the play into a spirit of revenge against their sister for contravening what they saw as her duty as a young widow. Bosola wants to avenge himself against the Cardinal and Ferdinand for 'neglect' and for forcing guilt upon him. Julia wants to revenge herself against the Cardinal for what she realises instinctively as his growing boredom of her. Antonio sees the Cardinal as his last recourse for revenge; his 'Could I take him At his prayers' (V.4.423) has its parallel in Shakespeare with Hamlet's regard for Claudius. The Cardinal avenges himself, by a blasphemous poisoning of his Holy Bible, against Julia because, rather like Eve's ascendancy over Adam, she acquires knowledge which damns him and then her. Ferdinand, in a white heat of rage, wants to avenge himself on the Cardinal for being coldly patronising throughout his life and enforcing his isolation whilst deranged. Bosola talks about the revenge he will wreak in Milan, though we are left in doubt about whether this is against Antonio (for past slights) or against the murdering brothers of the Duchess. A case can even be made out for the courtiers revenging themselves against the Cardinal, failing to come to his rescue when he was in trouble (and obviously not dissembling anymore), because of self-disgust at being diminished into the role of mere panders and flatterers of such arrogant princes.

TRAGEDY

Webster wrote his tragedies within an accepted classical tradition. As its characteristics it had: five acts, often with both a dumb-show and a play-within-a-play; continual recounting of off-stage horror and violence; a matched language of considerable brutishness; and all the action climaxing into an unhappy end. These 'tragedies of blood' commonly dwelt on the idea of revenge, incorporating ghosts, madness, dismembering and death. An almost organic concept within **tragedy** is the combination of pity and fear, epitomised in this play by character interplay; between the Duchess and her brothers and, in the end, Bosola and the Duchess.

The Duchess of Malfi incorporates **comedy** and death in what has been termed a significant comi-tragic relationship of 'laughing together'; a play where tragedy marches with and overcomes the humour of comic **satire**, where a corrupt society reflects the tragic goodness of the heroine and purposefully misunderstands that goodness, rejects those values for itself and prefers to adopt a lie. Such a standpoint leads inexorably to darkness, confusion and exhaustion: Ferdinand's 'sleep'. Tragedy is inevitable after that.

Yet at the very human centre of it is restorative insight. The Duchess is all too human. She displays unattractive characteristics: lust, disregard for her princely duties, deviousness, false accusation of her inferiors, greed, a questionable judgement (in her choice of Antonio), blasphemy (cursing God) and passive abuse in the possible neglect of her oldest son. She is the personification of tragedy, a tragic figure who rises to look tragedy firmly in the eye.

UNORTHODOX MARRIAGE

Much of the action of the play stems from the Duchess's unconventional but quite legal relationship with Antonio. As a lawyer Webster likes to present, in an unbiased way, both sides of an argument. That inevitably means that some of the moral issues remain unresolved. He gains particular satisfaction in having his characters run against the tide by flaunting orthodoxy, even if his own personal views are entirely conventional. The Duchess's marriage to Antonio is unconventional and improper to the point of attracting moral censure in at least three ways; it is unequal, it is secret and it is her second.

UNEQUAL
To marry 'out of class', particularly for a woman, was a social misdemeanour for the Elizabethans and Jacobeans. It was considered more acceptable for a man to marry below himself, drawing his wife up to his own level of social status, because as a married woman she had very

few rights, of property or otherwise. For a woman to marry 'below' herself, as in the Duchess's case to marry a servant, meant that her husband was ennobled to her status, causing envy and confusion amongst her peers and dissent amongst those lower on the social scale. It was therefore an imperative for her to maintain transparent propriety. This was acknowledged by Antonio when talking about his wife to Delio on the latter's return from a long absence in Rome, 'The common rabble do directly say / She is a strumpet ... [your graver heads] ... do observe I grow to infinite purchase / The left-hand way' (III.1.25–9).

Antonio is ultimately empowered by the Duchess, but most reluctantly, 'I do here put off all vain ceremony, / And only do appear to you, a young widow / That claims you for her husband' (I.2.372–4).

Assertive women provoked much controversy. Webster and his contemporaries had a recent and poignant example of that in the last Tudor monarch, Elizabeth. But even after the time of Elizabeth, who kept her throne intact by a combination of ever-watchful manipulativeness and a vow to remain single, women remained unemancipated.

SECRET
The clandestine nature of the Duchess and Antonio's marriage is unacceptable to their contemporaries because although, as we have examined, legal, it is presumed to be problematic for being private. The Council of Trent formalised the position of the Catholic Church; a promise or betrothal had no need of outside consent, witnesses or a priest for its validity. But such a union was not to be consummated until after a priest-administered sacramental act. The Cardinal, as an instrument of divine justice, is bound to uphold that principle. Webster cannot of course resist the opportunity to expose the Cardinal's hypocrisy (with Julia) but that in a way is beside the point.

Secrecy, once embarked upon, becomes a pattern. It is that secrecy, about the marriage and its outcomes in the children, that becomes destructive, leading to deception, false and undignified accusations by the Duchess and Antonio of the court officers; destructive ultimately of the marriage itself.

The secrecy that the Duchess practises is frowned on, too, because it flouts familial authority, conceals from the state facts it needs to know (not least to secure peaceful succession), and excludes that vital ingredient of priestly sacrament. Secrecy may not be morally aberrant, but it is repugnant and dangerous. Romantic love, flying in the face of good order, is, in **Renaissance** culture, an alien myth.

REMARRIAGE
Part of the Church's sacramental attitude to marriage infers its indissolubility, 'till death'. Webster implies a convenient application of this principle to both parties. Certainly Catholic teaching blurred the distinction between remarriage and bigamy. Ferdinand goes well beyond legal rectitude by referring to the Duchess's children as 'bastards' (IV.1.36) and doubting whether they have ever been christened (III.3.64). But contemporary religious dogma urged widows towards perpetual chastity and against the dangers of unbridled lust. Widows were assumed to be somewhere in that uncomfortable no-man's land of carnal knowledge (which made them, for instance, unacceptably aware in a convent) and awakened purity, which paradoxically made them unquestionably suitable for sex.

Remarriage also opened for the Aragon brothers a dilemma of inheritance. There is no question of their having any valid entitlement to the wealth and estates that went with the Dukedom of Malfi. That came to the dowager Duchess through her late, first, husband, and that right she held in trust until the majority (coming of age) of their son – a figure, some critics suggest, strangely neglected by Webster in the final scene. But there is also no doubt that Ferdinand, in particular, had designs upon those estates, even if illegally. He admits as much, mixed with his remorse, to Bosola at her death, 'I had a hope, / Had she continu'd widow, to have gain'd / An infinite mass of treasure by her death' (IV.2.277–9).

In Webster's time most widows did not remarry; wealthy widows even less – not least because, for the first time in their lives, they found themselves truly independent with the means to enjoy it, their identity no longer derived from either father or husband. The vitality of the Duchess's passion drove her to challenge conventional chastity; yet build a beneficial and fruitful marriage. That the marriage was marred and ultimately destroyed neither prevents it being initially benign for the Duchess, nor that out of it could not come, despite all the court disapproval and fraternal cruelty, her serenity even when in the very jaws of vicious death.

A WORD ABOUT INCEST AND FORNICATION

At first glance these perversions of love seem to have nothing to do with marriage, even marriage gone wrong. Nevertheless, they are the sexual misdemeanours of which the two princely Aragon brothers are guilty.

The vehemence of Ferdinand's outrage at his sister's marriage surprises and then alarms even the Cardinal. His brother's coarse language, giving vent to his imagination, 'To see her in the shameful act of sin', his lust for blood that leads him to offer the familial and phallic poniard, all seem to point to his carnal and unfulfilled and ultimately insane desire for his sister. It is intriguing, surprising even, that this motif of incest is not made more explicit in the play.

Webster's Cardinal is not at liberty to marry even if, unlike his brother, he were able to bring his sexuality under control. He finds Julia, however, an enthusiastic if somewhat unsophisticated partner; her indiscretion is her final undoing. But their relationship is uncompromisingly portrayed by the playwright as greedy, then cold and unforgiving, in contrast to the idyllic tie of the Duchess and Antonio.

Even in their tenderer moments Julia and the Cardinal's affair is shown as shallow, brilliant and brittle. He is cynical and she is fickle. He mocks her with **satire**. 'Why do you weep? / Are tears your justification? The selfsame tears / Will fall into your husband's bosom, lady, / With a loud protestation that you love him / Above the world' (II.4.20–4). As soon as he is out of the room to allow her to converse with her husband's emissary, she shows she is not averse to Delio's advances. Progress for Delio is thwarted by interruption, but Julia's opportunity for fresh illicit love is transferred later into her single-minded seduction of Bosola.

No doubt Webster uses these contorted deviations of desire to ameliorate audience disapproval already settling on the Duchess for her disregard of social, sexual and religious convention.

COUNSEL / FLATTERY

Although Webster's main **protagonist** is the Duchess, he gives Antonio a substantial role as counsellor who, by his learning, earns intimacy with his female prince. This sort of relationship is echoed faintly elsewhere in the play; Delio as counsellor to Antonio (although more often he is placed in the role of commentating observer), Ferdinand and the Cardinal to the Duchess, Pescara to the Cardinal, the Doctor to Ferdinand, Cariola to the Duchess, the Duchess (less faintly) to Cariola (women stick together), and Bosola (as well as being soldier, **malcontent**, intelligencer and honest fool) to anyone who would heed and hire him!

Antonio is inferior in class to the court he serves but gains class by his learning. It is within the **Renaissance humanist** tradition that it is in absorbing scholarship that the road to improvement lies. Education is the passport to power. The only defence that the nobility had against an erosion of their influence by such a powerful force as this learning was to take the benefit of the counsel, but fend off dilution of the aristocracy by proscribing any interbreeding.

The Duchess is aware and frustrated by the hindrance that class presents to her desire for a different kind of relationship with Antonio. He can be intimate with her as an educated servant, forthright, critical even. But he knows what contravenes convention, he will not cross the barrier. The Duchess wants egalitarian status, tells him not to kneel, chides his exclamation of unworthiness, rues the class division that sets her apart, 'The misery of us, that are born great, / We are forc'd to woo, because none dare woo us ... we / Are forc'd to express our violent passions / In riddles' (I.2.357–62). And yet she affirms she speaks it 'without flattery'.

For Webster flattery is the obverse of counsel and pandering is condemned in the first Act by Antonio (who initially is a symbol of wisdom and justice). He tells Delio in glowing terms of his observations of the new regime in the French court, now a place of purity, where the King 'Quits first his royal palace / Of flatt'ring sycophants' (I.1.7–8). Antonio explains to Delio that this is achieved by 'a most provident Council, who dare freely / Inform him' (I.1.17–18). We see the glint in Antonio's eye, how he means this standard to be his in the service of the Duchess. And we see by contrast how Rome and its princes, the Aragon brothers and their courtiers, are infected by the cancer of corruption. Bosola is quick to appraise Antonio of this sickness of the state, personified most obviously in the Cardinal and Ferdinand, 'He and his brother are like plum trees, that grow / crooked over standing pools, they are rich, and o'erladen / with fruit, but none but crows, pies, and caterpillars feed / on them. Could I be but one of their flatt'ring panders, I would / hang on their ears like a horse-leech, till I were full' (I.1.49–53).

Bosola can only be a pale shadow of Antonio's role of counsellor. He is most evidently a **malcontent**. Malcontents have a parallel role to counsellors in **Renaissance** drama which is of fundamental significance – to unsettle the power of the corrupt by a mean, ruthless and blunt spirit which can often lead to real disorder rather than just a shift in the balance of individual power. But whether underlying structure is effected by the cynicism of the malcontent rather than just an undermining of individual corruption is a moot point.

What is sure is that as the Duchess is forced to change counsellors from Antonio to Bosola she moves from a source of confidential discretion to the devious corruption of secrecy. Bosola simply does not have the moral force to allow him to act in the disinterested manner required and so does not rate the role of counsellor very highly. He is disparaging of Cariola's service just before her murder and of Ferdinand's just after. The Cardinal debases the currency of the term further in the last act, referring to the deaths he 'counselled' and Julia tells the Cardinal just before her death how she has 'counselled' Bosola to underhandedness. Once again, we are observers of the manner in which, from time to time, Webster wryly subverts values.

And sets them to right again. There are few more moving examples in the play of selfless counselling than the Duchess's of Cariola when they are under house arrest and facing death – a demonstration of how women of virtue support each other.

RELIGION / POLITICS

In theory religion is concerned with the dimension of a human being's spiritual relationship with the supernatural. Politics, by contrast, concerns human beings' interaction with each other, their government and authority structures. In practice, Webster draws these ideas close together and it is difficult to distinguish where one ends and the other takes on.

On the face of it the main characters are all secular except the Cardinal, and he seems to have developed some experience and skill in war before being made a Prince of the Church. Half way through the action of the play, the Holy Roman Emperor recruits the Cardinal back into his army as a soldier. In a ceremony in Loretto, the Cardinal resigns his priestly role and, although continuing to be referred to as the Cardinal, he effectively becomes secular again.

Even the Pope, overtly a religious leader, has a great deal of political power. He is not only head of a Europe-wide church, he is head of state (of the Vatican), has his own army and is heavily involved in lay politics. In the ceremony at Loretto the two pilgrims comment on the way the Church and the State act in concert concerning the Duchess; how the Cardinal has had her banished from Ancona, a state directly under the control of the Pope; and how the Pope, acting on rumours of the Duchess's 'looseness', dispossesses her of her dukedom. By what law, by what authority, by what justice, asks one of the pilgrim observers? To which the other replies, by none. The implication is that the Church has authority to act quixotically in whatever way it prefers. Church complicity and corruption become associated with the essential prerequisites and ingredients of power.

Webster understands that English sensibilities will be scandalised by this sort of arbitrary behaviour. More than half a century has passed since Henry VIII's excommunication by the Pope, and although the English court under Elizabeth was far from embracing any kind of Puritanism, it espoused the independence of the Church of England fiercely.

Politics, of course, is both a public and a private matter. In the public domain, the Aragon brothers believe the Duchess to be neglectful of her duties. She finds the affairs of state irksome and wills herself to be a commoner. Courtiers move up and down the pecking order by flattery (look at the fawning behaviour of Castruchio and Malateste) or straightforward honesty. Antonio and Pescara are among those held out as good examples of the latter.

Italy was a useful and neutral venue in which to site a play of intrigue; neutral because, although the issues and abuses Webster deals with are glaringly present in the English court, the distancing of them and their placing into a foreign setting was thought to offer the playwright some protection from a charge of anti-patriotism or treason.

Privately, politics is about insinuation. Bosola is deep into scheming, much of it to do with recovering what he sees as his neglected 'courtly reward' for past if illegal services to Ferdinand and the Cardinal. Interestingly it is Bosola who brings together the themes of religion and politics most convincingly. He has long given up any hope of receiving his just deserts for a lifetime of inveigling himself into the princes' service as executioner and demeaning intelligencer. He knows he is the villain bought to conduct vicarious murder and he comes to exact that reward by the killing of a Cardinal he once cynically invested with 'divinity' (I.1.41). This same Cardinal tries to buy a life, his own, and is met by Bosola's contemptuous rejection of his worth as either priest or politician, 'Thy prayers and proffers / Are both unseasonable … Pray, and be sudden: when thou kill'd'st thy sister, / Thou took'st from Justice her most equal balance, / And left her naught but her sword' (V.5.15–16, 38–40).

The audience will register shock at how the Duchess confuses the boundaries of religion and politics, too. Bosola attempts to stimulate her faith in her last hour by reminding her that 'You are a Christian' (IV.1.75). For her, a realistic fatalism is more reassuring. Hope left undisturbed cannot disappoint.

Cariola, however, is shown as overtly pious. She is critical of her mistress for turning a pilgrimage to Loretto into a means of escape. She attempts to delay execution by saying she is unshriven. Her religion will be seen by the audience as conformist superstition.

Paradoxically, true religion is probably best interpreted, **humanistically**, by Antonio's **simile** for politics and good government; 'a Prince's court / Is like a common fountain, whence should flow / Pure silver-drops in general. But if't … poison't near the head,/ Death and diseases through the whole land spread' (I.1.11–15).

CONFINEMENT

Over centuries of performance audiences have often found this play claustrophobic. Much of the action takes place in confined spaces, a **metaphor** indeed for the theatre space itself. Throughout most of the drama there is an atmosphere of threat. On the few occasions where a scene is set in a more open space, for example when the Duchess flees from Ancona with her diminished entourage or when Antonio and Delio approach the Cardinal's quarters in Milan by night, menace is still palpable; in the first instance, she is arrested, and in the second the ghostly echo bombards them with doom. A sense of entrapment, the enclosedness of the play, is most experienced by themes of prison, madness and, sometimes, marriage.

Prison is where the Duchess nearly always is throughout the drama. She is at court, alone, and her brothers intend to keep her there. Escaping from them and into Antonio's world is ultimately futile. She has one determined attempt at freedom, sending Antonio to Ancona and planning to join him nearby at Loretto. She nearly succeeds but, in confiding her plans to Bosola and accepting his assistance, her vulnerable openness proves to be a fatal trap.

What she learns, to her lasting credit, is that even under house arrest she may win a degree of independence and freedom; so that she can turn this idea of confinement on its head and say to Cariola, when their privacy is invaded by the madmen, 'nothing but noise, and folly / Can keep me in my right wits, whereas reason / And silence make me stark mad' (IV.2.5–7). She is realistic enough to know, however, that such a dark confining prison will inevitably kill the spirit, 'The robin red-breast and the nightingale / Never live long in cages' (IV.2.13–14).

When the Duchess comes to die, Bosola introduces her to her greatest confinement, her smallest last benefit, her coffin. 'This is your last presence chamber' he says. (IV.2.168). The Duchess, however, is conscious of a narrowing of her perspective in order to gain something much wider. As she submits to her horrible, asphyxiating death, she kneels because 'heaven gates are not so highly arch'd / As princes' palaces: they that enter there / Must go upon their knees' (IV.2.228–30).

Sometimes madness is more entertaining for the insane than for those who come to observe. Not least does this apply to lovers, so bound up in their obsession that they seem for all the world deranged. Thus does Cariola conclude, watching Antonio and the Duchess in a tryst confined to her chamber, 'A fearful madness: I owe her much of pity' (I.2.419).

There is no doubt what the Duchess's brothers think of such unalloyed and uncareful love. They advise her before they know about her affair with Antonio that they know about her tendency towards disorder, 'You live in a rank pasture here', and that 'The marriage night / Is the entrance into some prison' (I.2.227, 243–4).

The Duchess makes great play of giving her wedding ring to Antonio. By it, of course, she entraps him as her husband. They both know it as a **metaphor** for her femininity. Meanwhile he must have given her another one, or reinvested her with the first. Because at Loretto one pilgrim asks the other what it was that the Cardinal removed so violently from her finger; to receive the response that it was a wedding ring, a symbol of revenge. Thus confinement and revenge are seen alike as constricting; the Cardinal, in removing the sign to him of the one, binds himself to the other. Much later the ring is purportedly given back to the Duchess by Ferdinand on the finger of the dismembered dead man's hand.

The mad are doubly confined, within their fantasies and within their hospital. They are used by Ferdinand to torture his twin sister, 'To bring her to despair' (IV.1.115). He wants to reinforce her consciousness of her restriction by their restriction. She admits to his servant that she is 'chain'd to endure all your tyranny' (IV.2.61) and yet claims it is the very noise of their mental assault of her that she finds remedial. When they have finished and Bosola, disguised as an old man, enters she cannot refrain from the wry question as to the state of his sanity too. Indeed we may echo the observation implied in her question. How can a human being do what he has to do and remain sane? But Bosola seems made of sterner stuff than Ferdinand.

The Duchess finds a rest in sleep which she knows instinctively will quickly turn to death. After raging against their sister to his brother, which alarms the Cardinal to admonish 'You fly beyond your reason', Ferdinand also promises, 'I'll go sleep: / Till I know who leaps my sister, I'll not stir' (II.5.77–8), a sleep which quickly turns for him into a peculiar kind of schizophrenia. Yet even in that madness is a peculiar kind of insight; he asks his courtiers to protect him from the doctor 'Physicians are like kings, / They brook no contradiction' (V.2.64–5), as he sees through hollow charlatanism 'there's / nothing left of you, but tongue and belly, flattery and / lechery' (V.2.78–80).

In the end, just as Ferdinand's hate of his sister flows out of his frustrated and aberrant love for her, so his madness flows inevitably out of that hate. This, in its turn, can only lead into a confinement of isolation that the brotherly care of the Cardinal insists upon. For Ferdinand the only exit available from that trap is the violence of death, as almost his final words confirm 'I will vault credit, and affect high pleasures / Beyond death' (V.5.67–8).

Madness is a tool playwrights use to introduce taboo subjects, a device to get round the censor. The prime task of the censor, of course, is to confine.

OTHER THEMES

SIN
We have examined specifically carnal sins, but sin as a doctrine features throughout, partly as an example of the weakness of the human condition, and partly as a moralistic warning of pitfalls to avoid. Witness the brothers' **imagery** in their early admonition of their sister not to fall into the habit of lusty widows, 'Their livers are more spotted / Than Laban's sheep'. In the same breath they talk of witchcraft and deviltry, and hypocritically of how such 'Will come to light'. 'Lustful pleasures', they say 'forerun man's mischief' (I.2.219–20, 236, 245–6).

Who more appropriate than the Cardinal, senior member of the family, to spell out the dogma 'Sorrow is held the eldest child of sin' (V.5.54)?

IDENTITY
This at first seems peculiarly relevant to the Duchess who, along with her brother the Cardinal, is given no other name by the playwright. We may ask why this is so? Somehow it distances her from us. Not only her nobility but her lack of a forename puts her beyond our reach. We have sympathy for an Antonio who becomes her lover/husband but never seems to be able to cross that paradox/divide into a familiarity and familialness which goes with a patrician no-naming.

Strangely, even her brothers, intimates from childhood, refer to her directly as you and, in her absence, as the Duchess, or with increasing contempt as sister, strumpet, curs'd creature and so on. No wonder she enters an identity crisis of her own when, faced with the disguised old man of death (Bosola), she challenges him to name her, 'Dost know me?' then 'Who am I?' through 'Am not I thy Duchess?' to a final and resigned affirmation 'I am Duchess of Malfi still' (IV.2.120, 122, 132, 139). So that for all her expressions of intent to Antonio at a levelling, she retreats finally into an identity of position rather than personality. Once the Duchess has lost her status, she does not know who she is, so that she can question with apparent innocence 'Are you not my brother?' But still turn that innocuousness on its head with the bitingly dismissive answer she provides for herself, 'No you are a villain'.

Anonymity is akin to a denial of identity for the Duchess, and she fights it as much as Ferdinand welcomes it for the concealing darkness that accompanies it. Bosola demands it as disguise, courtiers appear in masques and even weapons are rarely naked.

THE FUTILITY OF GREATNESS / THE DECADENCE OF HIGH LIFE / UNIVERSAL MORTALITY

Instances will be found throughout the play to illustrate these interrelated ideas.

The futility of greatness is well observed, and particularly in the character assassination by Bosola of his masters. Without too fully engaging in the detail of this, he refers to them as rich but providing food for none but crows (I.1.51). The audience may conjecture the **irony** that the fruit that comes from their crooked and fetid growth is not unlike in quality the fruit that Bosola is soon to present to the Duchess which leads to her illness and inexorably to her undoing.

Bosola and Antonio's discussion focuses on mortality, and how it applies even to those who aspire to be great. Hawks have reward, says Bosola, but all that soldiers receive is injury, procession from one hospital to another and in the end being laid out head to foot, in coffins.

One of the features of a **tragedy** is that all the major characters, high and low, die. Most poignantly is this expressed by the Cardinal in his final breath, 'And now, I pray, let me / Be laid by, and never thought of' (V.5.88–9).

High life and decadence may not only be observed, most obviously, in the experience of the Cardinal; his adulterous relationship with Julia and the alacrity with which he dispenses with his cardinal's habit for a soldier's armour. It can be seen in the style of life and flatteringly extravagant language of the courtiers, with the notable exception of Pescara. Traces of decadence are apparent, too, in less likely places, not so exalted. Delio seems affected by its infection, as we have seen, not least in his rather ignominious suggestion to Julia that she become his mistress again (II.4.74).

Julia, of course, is only 'high life' by association, being married to
Castruchio who is a minor courtier. She is however decadent through and
through. For much of the play she is the Cardinal's lover. She
coquettishly tells Delio she must ask her husband's leave to switch her
favours to him. And slides on down the social scale, from Antonio's
bosom friend to end up, potentially, even if the relationship never gets
physical, as mistress of ex-galley slave Bosola.

The most futile of noble figures in the play is also the most tragic.
The Duchess confesses to Antonio 'The misery of us, that are born great,
/ We are forc'd to woo, because none dare ...' (I.2.357–8). At least a
counsellor's improvement was assured to him by his education. There was
nowhere for the Duchess to go. The pilgrims in Ancona discuss how her
brothers override the law to have her banished, how the Pope sets justice
aside to have her disinherited (III.4.30–2). Even her palace becomes her
prison and as Bosola calls her 'your Grace' she scorns his subservience,
'why dost thou wrap thy poison'd pills / In gold and sugar?' (IV.1.19–20).
Finally, his disguise allows him to pronounce a brutal truth 'Thou art
some great woman, sure ...'(IV.2.133). But, he insinuates, you are
prematurely grey, you cannot sleep at peace and your glory is 'like glow-
worms, afar off shine bright, / But look'd to near, have neither heat not
light' (IV.2.141–2). By then, of course, he has become her tomb-maker,
common bellman and chief executioner.

SEEMING

As the play proceeds with deadly logic towards its bloody end, its
characters become increasingly unsure of who or where they are. This is
well summed up by Bosola, dying as the courtiers finally pluck up courage
to break in on the final scene of carnage and ask how matters have come
to such a state. 'In a mist: I know not how; / Such a mistake as I have
often seen / In a play' (V.5.93–5).

Part of the dramatist's skill is to build a credible confusion in the
minds of his audience, and then to unpack that confusion so carefully as
to make things 'seem' what they are not, to show how the impossible may
be magically transformed to the probable.

So that, for the Duchess, it seems – by the dead man's hand, by
the waxwork figures, by false reports – that her husband Antonio is dead.
So that it seems that the people let loose on her in her house-arrest are

deranged, but perhaps, the audience may wonder, these people are masking madness at the whim of Duke Ferdinand. So that we see the upright honesty of Antonio and then his apparent cowardice in the face of danger. So that it seems, at the start of the play, that we can know, without a hint of uncertainty, that the Cardinal and Ferdinand and Bosola are unremittingly evil and Antonio and Delio are unswervingly good. And yet we are allowed to witness the Cardinal's remorse, and Ferdinand's partial return to sanity and Bosola's vain attempt to save Antonio. We see Antonio discredit authority and undermine power so that only anarchy can possibly prevail, and we see Delio, himself an ambiguous figure and not averse to a dabble at dissembling, return as kingmaker and install Antonio's heir as the Duchess's heir, 'Let us make noble use / Of this great ruin; and join all our force / To establish this young hopeful gentleman / In's mother's right ... I have ever thought / Nature doth nothing so great for great men, / As when she's pleas'd to make them lords of truth' (V.5.109–18).

The **irony** is that we are left wondering whether Delio is doing right by the Duchess and his friend Antonio and their son and himself, at the expense of the son of the Duchess's first husband. Even the 'seeming', it seems, has to make way in the end for what seems to be, not what is.

CORRUPTION
Many of the themes we have touched on may be summarised in the idea of corruption: corruption of settled order as well as corruption of ideals:
• Antonio rejects the poison the French court has rid itself of (I.1.12–14)
• Bosola despises the crooked ways of the Cardinal and Duke Ferdinand (I.1.49–50)
• Antonio rues that rust has entered into Bosola's soul (I.1.78)
• Bosola recognises that his own corruption 'Grew out of horse dung' (I.2.207–8)
• Bosola admits to the Old Lady that even good fruit rots in time (II.2.17)
• Ferdinand confesses that princes' palaces have a 'pestilent air' (III.1.50)
• Antonio describes Ferdinand's behaviour as rotten 'in his rank gall' (III.2.154)

- Bosola describes the work of informers as 'men that paint weeds' (III.2.329)

And so on. Readers of this Note are invited to complete the list. You will find that hardly a scene goes by without further examples.

CHARACTERISATION

THE DUCHESS

What makes the Duchess such a compelling stage presence is what one critic refers to as her 'strength … in weakness'. She cannot win against her all-powerful awful brothers and yet she is 'Duchess of Malfi still' (IV.2.139).

Webster gives us no absolute guidance to settle our opinions as to her character and personality. She is a hero with significant flaws. Antonio reiterates (with a perverse pride?) the rabble's estimation that 'she is a strumpet' (III.1.26). Ferdinand, with the **irony** of insightful acuity, thinks of her as a **Renaissance** stereotype 'lusty widow' (I.2.259).

Most critics are unsympathetic of her seemingly duplicitous response to her brothers' demand that she remain a widow, 'I'll never marry —' (I.2.223), and thereby miss Webster's subtlety. Ferdinand has been cross-questioning her, excitedly; he is cross that she argues back. In exasperation he almost shouts 'Will you hear me?' and cuts her off before she can finish her sentence. Notice the dash after her last word, marry, as her brother interjects with 'So most widows say'. Webster gives us no hint of what she would have said had she continued. But it is reasonable to assert that this truncated statement is poor evidence for her supposed deception.

The Duchess is in fact consistently open and direct. She is lusty and knows it; shows it to Antonio in their bedroom in a riposte full of sexual **innuendo**, 'What pleasure can two lovers find in sleep?' (III.2.10). She is only mildly more modest to Ferdinand in defence of her marriage, 'I have youth / And a little beauty' (III.2.139–40).

Her attitude to religion and the Church is ambivalent. She is dismissive of what she sees as the superficial and credulous practices of its adherents; for instance when her maid is critical of her projected and feigned pilgrimage to Loretto she instinctively admonishes Cariola as a 'superstitious fool' (III.2.317). Yet at the moment of her violent death she faces heaven calmly, knowing that 'they that enter there / Must go upon their knees' (IV.2.229–30).

What some critics have seen as her boldness and impetuosity, in her determination to marry, in her choice of husband, in her desire to live life away from the limelight in an abdication of her responsibility to exercise authority, in her denial of the advantages of birth and thus to 'put off all vain ceremony' (I.2.372), we may perceive as undeniable strength. She has a more dominant will than any who surround her. She wants to remarry. She decides her husband will be her steward. She wants children, and is skilful enough to produce them whilst still concealing their existence. When her cover is blown and her brother learns of her 'disobedience', she very nearly escapes.

Only Bosola is ever a match for her, and only he sometimes. It is true he tricks her into captivity, but in the end he has to acknowledge her worth, her innocence and 'behaviour so noble, / As gives a majesty to adversity' (IV.1.5–6), and confirms Antonio's opinion made at the start of her 'such noble virtue' (I.2.123).

Others have insinuated that it is her very probity that is the cause of disharmony around her court. It seems churlish to blame an unblemished soul for the manner in which evil forces react to her goodness. And yet this is Ferdinand's implication in his dying words, 'My sister, oh! my sister, there's the cause on't' (V.5.70).

For the Duchess, the greatest agony is darkness; she curses the night stars, the Russian winter (IV.1.94, 97); she experiences her twin brother move about her in a black disguise of darkness. Through it and isolation she grows into a peaceable acceptance. All her qualities are concentrated in her death. She has had to submit in order to rule.

BOSOLA

Bosola is a loner. He carries the loneliness of a man everyone has come to realise cannot be trusted. He is at heart the ultimate servant, the quintessential intelligencer.

Antonio defines him as a 'black malcontent' (I.1.80) whose 'foul melancholy / Will poison all his goodness' (I.1.75–6).

Webster enjoys a **pun** on his name. 'Bos' can mean a protuberance on a body, a prominence or knob; or sometimes it indicates an enlarged part of a shaft, or a conduit running out of the belly of a figure. It can also **ironically** be slang for masterliness. And 'ola' is the diminutive; both definitions a nice paradox for this quintessential servant.

Bosola shares an identity as **malcontent** with other dramatic Jacobean figures like Ford's Vasquez, and Middleton and Rowley's De Flores. A malcontent has knowledge and intelligence without status. Bosola begins as almost honest rough, an innocent lamb amongst predatory wolves (Act I Scene 1). He is aware that his lot is always to be bought, and turns bitter at a lack of necessities; 'Let good men, for good deeds, covet good fame, / Since place and riches oft are bribes of shame' (I.2.210–11). He recognises the base quality of being an intelligencer; 'my corruption / Grew out of horse dung' (I.2.207–8). And he knows that to be successful he must be clever, 'to avoid ingratitude / For the good deed you have done me, I must do / All the ill man can invent' (I.2.194–6).

Unlike the Duchess, he has learnt there are some battles you can never win, a lesson reinforced the hard way by spending some years in a galley ship. He claims he has performed this 'service' on behalf of the Cardinal. As Delio confides the rumour to Antonio, Bosola has been serving time as punishment for a commissioned murder.

Whatever the circumstances, Bosola is locked into a cycle of working for corrupt and powerful masters. This is his living, and his knowledge of it and competence at it give him power. He is unambitious for status, is discreet when it suits him and his silence cannot be bought. He is an employee, but he will not submit.

His work as intelligencer/spy/mercenary/hit-man means he is trusted by no one. To trust him, even for a moment, is fatal. It is the Duchess's tragic mistake. She is so soothed by his surprising praise of Antonio that she confides in him her innermost secret and asks him to secrete her wealth out to Antonio. He repays her confidence by betrayal and larceny. His final service to his mistress is to have her strangled.

He is never afraid, but ever feared, even by so cool a cleric as the Cardinal. Meantime, as the universal servant he is useful. It is a role he knows instinctively. He is in fact so used to being useful he serves both Duchess and her brothers simultaneously, holding such conflicts of interest with untroubled composure. His servanting does not have room

for morals or finer feelings. He is neither villain nor hero, he is angry at
being victim, he is careful and full of angst, his intrinsic intellect always
busy looking for the next main chance for well-rewarded labour. He
typifies the bright working-class boy who finds himself in an upper-class
world without the polish to handle the unspoken rules smoothly enough.
He thinks he is right and, very much like a performing dog with a strange
master, keeps getting confused.

Sometimes we are entitled to wonder whether Webster is
attempting to portray Bosola with an awakening conscience, particularly
after the Duchess's death, when in Act V he **soliloquises** about Antonio's
plight. But we cannot be certain about his motives even then towards his
late mistress's husband as he sets his face towards his final mission; to kill
or to save Antonio? 'I'll post to Milan, / Where somewhat I will speedily
enact / Worth my dejection' (IV.2.367–9).

In the end he does kill him; we are led to believe, unintentionally.
But we are not quite sure, just as we cannot be convinced about anything
about Bosola. Certainly, Antonio's death is as convenient as, shortly
before, Julia's murder by the Cardinal was. After all, Antonio had been a
rival servant. And the Cardinal, in a grizzly pact, had commissioned the
death of the Duchess's husband; and presumably would pay. To the
Cardinal's simple question, 'Thou wilt kill Antonio?' there had been a
simple reply, 'Yes'. To do less would be a falling short of the high
standards of good stewardship.

Bosola, in the last analysis, is a tragic figure. 'I am your creature'
(I.2.208) he panders to the Duke. He is spy and intelligencer; he is also
intelligent – witness his clever scheme to trick the Duchess with the
apricots. He is faithful, but his faithfulness is to tyranny (IV.2.323).
Antonio, who divined good in the Cardinal, perceived 'goodness' in
Bosola too (I.1.76), evidence for this being in his rejection of Ferdinand's
worst excesses after the waxwork torture of the Duchess, 'go no farther in
your cruelty' (IV.1.116). In truth because he is neglected and discarded he
is dangerous because still dynamic. Delio suggests that he is too studious,
'a fantastical scholar' (III.3.40), an echo, perhaps, of Marlowe's Faustus.
But in his appetite for learning it seems it is not knowledge that Bosola
seeks but appearances, 'to gain the / name of a speculative man'
(III.3.45–6). And when the last of his masters, the Cardinal, is 'in some
disgrace / With the Emperor', Bosola is like a rat that leaves the sinking

ship, 'like the mice / That forsake falling houses, I would shift / To other dependence' (V.2.202–5). Even Julia's seducing of him fails because he is too bound up with his drive to serve; he is grateful to the Cardinal when she as distraction is removed, 'Believe me, you have done a very happy turn' (V.2.321).

Bosola's is a more dispassionate **solipsism** than Ferdinand's. For an 'intelligencer' people are pawns; women seem hardly more than objects and for men there is a hatred brought about by pure envy of his fellows' grace. So the revenger is doomed, killing whom he would have saved, not even rewarded by being the arm 'that strikes / With the sword of justice' (V.2.339–40), realising his is just a part in Webster's **irony**, 'lastly, for myself, / That was an actor in the main of all, / Much 'gainst mine own good nature, yet i'th' end / Neglected' (V.5.83–6): His final and highest aim, to be a noble actor.

THE CARDINAL

> 'You enforce your merit too much' (I.1.34)
>
> 'Let me be laid by, and never thought of' (V.5.88–9)

The first thought has an unpleasant way of being overtaken by the last. Both phrases are the Cardinal's and between them the audience has witnessed a play whose forces ebb and flow and make this aristocratic autocrat by turns powerful, frightened and ultimately extinguished.

Some critics see the Cardinal's cold and calculating cruelty as the antithesis of Ferdinand's hot and evil impetuosity. The older brother is passionless in achieving his personal ambitions and in the treatment of his sister. His career moves are executed with clinical precision; from Duke (before the play begins) to Cardinal to soldier. He helps himself to pleasure from his mistress without offering her anything of himself. He gives her death. He gives no one more.

The play starts with his presence commanding attention. The play ends by his willing himself into oblivion. At the beginning, Bosola describes the two Aragon brothers at court as 'crooked' (I.1.50). This contrasts with Antonio's view of the French court as 'Pure silver' (I.1.13). Antonio moreover, although disapproving of the Cardinal's worldliness as portrayed by Delio, his sombreness mixed with subterfuge and conspiratorial corruption, concedes he has done 'Some good' (I.2.89). After listing a litany of negatives, this positive is unconvincing. Indeed, we get little inkling of it in the play. Antonio may be speaking ironically; certainly he comments to Delio that the brothers are twins 'In quality' (I.2.94), a timely reminder that although Ferdinand and the Duchess are twins in nature, Ferdinand and the Cardinal share base qualities of badness, the madness of the first seeping into the second, diluted; evidence being the frenetic and disorganised manner in which he sets about Antonio's murder.

He is surprisingly young for the role of Christian Prince which a cardinalship bestows. If the Duchess is about nineteen years old when the play opens, then so is Ferdinand. And although the Cardinal is older, there is a limit to how much older he can be. The temporal power of a Dukedom in the kind of theocracy which subsists is inevitably subservient to Church power; and the Cardinal is temperamentally disinclined to subservience.

An icy ruthlessness epitomises all the Cardinal's actions. He uses his 'perverse and turbulent' brother to dispose of their sister. He discards his mistress by a grotesque and blasphemous murder. He seems incapable of guilt or remorse, at least until after his disloyal but obedient courtiers have failed to protect him from Bosola, their undutifulness articulated by Roderigo, 'I'll see him hang'd, ere I'll go down to him' (V.5.22). Then can he utter 'Sorrow is held the eldest child of sin' (V.5.54). Towards the end we see him studious over religious dogma 'puzzl'd in a question' (V.5.1). He is thinking about hell. But not as a possible destination or as a place he personally deserves. Conscience is tedious. To be set aside.

FERDINAND

Is Ferdinand the younger twin? Bosola pretends to assume that this must be so from his conversation with the Duke (IV.2.261–3) soon after the Duchess's death; earlier, he has referred to Ferdinand, whilst talking to the Duchess, as 'Your elder brother' (IV.1.21).

Webster breathes into this brother a capacity for intensity; love and hate. Early on, he is seen as inadequate, has that detachment twins sometimes display to the world 'outside', becoming alienated and incapable of reciprocation, and shows the unresolved displacement of a middle sibling. He lacks the natural authority which is the birthright of the first-born and is keenly aware of the spoiltness he is denied not being the youngest. He only fills the title of Duke by default. His older brother has grown tired of it, accepting a cardinal's hat which gives him license to practice politics on a far wider scale.

Although Webster gives Ferdinand a primary part in the play, he does not lack insight into his secondary position in the family. His feelings of inadequacy lead him into a hectoring spirit, which in turn leads to isolation, and then to savagery. Savagery for him ends in madness. Such a progression in the loss of conventional inhibition is going to be the path we trace for Ferdinand.

We can only surmise his real motives for wishing his sister not to remarry and a subsequent willing of her death. After he has had her killed he tells Bosola he had hoped 'to have gain'd / An infinite mass of treasure by her death' (IV.2.278–9). This sounds an unconvincing piece of obfuscation and we have every right to reject it as spurious. For a start Ferdinand rarely gives real reasons for his actions; he inhabits dark places where the light of truth is at best murky. And although his sister has by repute made Malfi prosperous he is lord of the much better endowed estates of Aragon, Calabria and Castile. Malfi is little more than a few poor fishing villages stretched out along a rugged coast – there is nothing easy or smooth about it like the great centres of learning, Naples, Rome or Milan. As a place it is worth nothing.

It may be jealousy but whatever Ferdinand's purpose, the thrust of his driving passion throughout the play is focused on his determination to control the Duchess; by disapproval of her, anger at her, and by an all-devouring love-turned-hate. The signs of this unnatural sexuality make fertile territory for conjecture by critics.

The indication is that Ferdinand is unmarried and without a lover and that he is tortuously inhibited. He exults in a voyeuristic description to his brother of his imaginative vision of their sister 'in the shameful act of sin' (II.5.41). In doing so he admits unconsciously to his own shameful act of pornographic voyeurism, defined by one critic as 'an heterosexual power relation with female submission as its precondition' (Simon Hardy).

In his hate Ferdinand is as ruthless as the Cardinal. But where the older brother is cold, the younger brother is hot. As has been noted, for a while he stifles any expression of his hatred. For a couple of Acts he feigns sleep, the only guardian of control. But all the time he is full of imprecation, he perambulates, a sort of restless sleep-walking, and by Act III he is desperate to seize the initiative. To cover his shame he approaches his sister in darkness and torments her with a progression of imported madnesses soon to overcome his own sensibility; a dead man's hand (IV.1.43), wax effigies (IV.1.55), intrusions by the seriously insane (IV.2.61). When she sleeps in a swoon of death he comes to her again. His eyes are dazzled at the sight of her, alive or dead (IV.2.259), and he must cover her at once; then, as distraction, 'go hunt the badger by owl-light: / 'Tis a deed of darkness' (IV.2.328–9).

Finally, dark madness invades his soul. Control is lost as he signals his transgression into gratuitous violence. He has grown so crooked he cannot recognise his colleague criminals as friends. So he stabs them as alien enemies. 'Strangling is a very quiet death' (V.4.33); his own demise is a raucous slide into **solipsism** when every last light is long extinguished.

Antonio

Stewards must have people skills. Antonio is basically a decent man but no match for the testing circumstances into which Webster pitches him. Bosola likens him to a 'cedar' (III.2.263) and therefore, by implication, judges him to be straight. Ferdinand glosses this by asserting that shaking a cedar makes it strong (I.2.163–4). The audience may interpret Antonio differently whilst employing the same image; that he is wooden, earnest and mildly humourless, and that the storm that comes to shake him unsteadies him.

The play opens with Antonio and his friend Delio as outsiders. As such they can comment dispassionately about corruption at the court from which they have become detached, and compare it with the purity and good order of the court in France, 'like a common fountain' (I.1.12).

Antonio is counsellor to the Duchess. The education necessary for that role has had the effect of raising his status to the level of her confidante, but he recognises he can never be her equal in blood. Even to aspire to it is a presumption he will not countenance, 'Ambition, Madam, is a great man's madness' (I.2.337). This, however, does not stop him hero-worshipping her, as he confides to Delio, 'For her discourse, it is so full of rapture, / You only will begin, then to be sorry / When she doth end her speech' (I.2.112–14). By the same token he is confused by her wooing of him and sees his own place in this as a dangerous gesture of defiance at her brothers. His consent, therefore, to the ensuing and secret marriage can be interpreted as more passive than resolute, and his new wife senses that more wooing is needed, post ceremony, before he will be able to perform any conjugal act. She gently suggests he lead her to the marriage bed to 'only lie, and talk together, and plot' (I.2.411).

Plotting is an activity he is uncomfortable with; his wife is more adept at it than he. She seems more manly too, more accustomed to taking the initiative in their moments of crisis. Before the birth of their first child he fails to protect her from Bosola's subterfuge by declining her wish to taste the apricots (II.1.146). Then he panics to Delio when her gluttony precipitates labour (II.1.164). After his wife's confinement he fails her again, dropping the horoscope evidence of the child's birth at Bosola's feet; and this was just the proof the intelligencer needed of the Duchess's 'disobedience' of her brothers' instructions. Antonio compounds his lack of vigilance by a clumsy blunder in an accusation of poisoning of the Duchess that Bosola is clearly innocent of. The scene between these two rivals for their mistress's confidence develops into a trading of insults. Perhaps it is only the open declaration of a long-festering dislike, initially as a result of rivalry over competing merits of horsemanship, but it ends for Antonio in an ignominious nose-bleed.

Antonio's juvenile game with Cariola makes the Duchess vulnerable again and presents Ferdinand with the opportunity of an unannounced visit to her room which serves to confirm his suspicions of what he sees as her duplicity. It is the Duchess who devises her family's escape from Malfi and it is Antonio who stands passively by as they are banished from Ancona at the shrine in Loretto. At their final parting, it is Antonio who deserts her to almost immediate arrest by Bosola as agent of her scheming brothers. She comments on his paralysis of fear which he confesses to before his peremptory flight, 'My heart is turn'd to a heavy lump of lead, / With which I sound my danger' (III.5.88–9).

He does not even seem to be pro-active enough to be in the way of hearing about her death, although it is carried out within the cognisance of a widening circle of collaborators. His efforts in Act V to attempt a reconciliation with the Duchess's murdering brothers would be hilarious were they not so contemptible. As it is these despicable brothers are dismissed as unworthy of Antonio's ploy by Delio, 'I cannot think they mean well to your life' (V.1.11).

Critics have seen Antonio as posing some sort of threat to Ferdinand and the Cardinal's hegemony in Malfi, and attribute this to accounting for their opposition to the Duchess's marriage. If this is so, the Aragon brothers much overrated the threat Antonio posed. In truth, he is shown to be weak from the beginning, though initially we may interpret this as gentlemanliness. It is only later that we come to recognise this characteristic as innate feebleness. Others may consider this opinion unfair, pointing out that the brave Duchess sees him as worthy. Is her judgement that secure? After all she appointed and confided in Bosola. Certainly Antonio is generous, quick to see good in those we dismiss as evil; he is modest, and honest, a scholar of history with a reverence for history (V.3.9), even if somewhat slow to apply the hard lessons it teaches.

As seems appropriate for this ineffective man, he dies in a casual anticlimax. His last thoughts are for his son's escape and to commend himself to his friend. This is hardly stirring stuff, and we are left with an impression of the emptiness of a life fuller of promise than performance, and which he himself, with an appropriate deprecation, describes: 'We follow after bubbles' (V.4.65).

DELIO

Antonio's friend; though for much of the play, when he isn't a kind of fringe-courtier, he acts as counsellor's counsellor. In fact his relationship with Antonio has parallels with Cariola's with the Duchess. They both advise; the difference being that Delio seems more intelligent than Antonio, but Cariola less so than the Duchess.

Delio and Antonio operate as a team throughout most of the play, though there are significant times when they are geographically apart. Often they seem to stand back from the action just to commentate, to help the audience jump the gaps, introduce more actors or understand the plot. When Antonio is down on his luck it is Delio who helps him plan and hopes with him to restore his fortunes. (We have already, in our study of the Duchess, come to realise that plotting is not Antonio's strength.) It is Delio who petitions Pescara for the citadel, it is Delio who accompanies Antonio to the Cardinal's apartment to try and effect a reconciliation and it is Delio who makes sure that Antonio's son succeeds to his inheritance, 'To establish this young hopeful gentleman / In's mother's right' (V.5.111–12).

But there is a cogent argument that Webster is more subtle with Delio than Shakespeare is with Horatio in *Hamlet*, because he endows him with a weakness, and therefore makes him theatrically more credible. In a moment of revealing self-interest, Delio attempts to take his lustful chance with Julia, her husband Castruchio impotent and in any case absent, and she out of favour with her Cardinal lover.

But he is a less skilful negotiator with women and after a truncated discourse of unconvincing courtship, his blunt suggestion that she become his mistress when she is free to do so is met with coquettish prevarication. She as courtesan is more than his courtly equal, which he ruefully acknowledges, and she declares she will have to ask permission, 'Sir, I'll go ask my husband if I shall' (II.4.75). In the meantime he gets absorbed back into the more staid affairs of state.

Antonio uses Delio as his intelligencer when the latter is in the company of the great in the centres of learning and influence, Naples, Rome and Milan. But he is not so effective in this role as Bosola. He is not only a less than admirable best friend; he is not very successful, failing to seduce Julia or to importune Pescara, over-concerned with rank and somewhat under-concerned about his friend's spouse. His name means, literally, I delete. He is adept at blotting out the uncomfortable. In Act V Scene 3 he conjures up the Duchess, bringing back an echo who has left the stage too soon; and then abandons her again. As readers we may feel he himself has as much substance as an echo. All ends well for him, however; installed in influence as regent Duke.

Somehow we do not part company with Delio with much regret. We wonder whether he has not been somewhat of a fair-weather friend. He is too much of a courtier, seems to have taken on their attributes of pandering and flattering. Cleverer and stronger than Antonio, he is never there when his friend needs him; when Antonio parts finally from the Duchess, and when Antonio is killed by Bosola.

JULIA

Events surrounding Julia comprise the subplot some producers of the play choose to cut. They cut a lot of fun, and not a little gore, and some delightfully plain and saucy speaking.

Webster integrates her so deftly into the plot to show the sick effeteness of the Court, the venal corruption of the Church and the paradox of women's informal power and formal powerlessness.

Julia is married to 'old' Castruchio, a minor nobleman with vane aspirations above his modest ability to serve as a judge. He hangs about at court, hoping to secure an appropriate appointment.

And neglects his lusty wife. 'Lusty' is an epithet already applied to the Duchess about which there may be some argument but there can be little about it applying to Julia. When the play begins she is the open mistress of a cardinal whose brother seems manically disorientated by conventional sex. Bullyingly, the Duke turns the power of this aversion against his Duchess sister rather than his Cardinal older brother.

And as spectators we get to overhear Julia's pillow-talk. She is good at it and the Church is discredited thereby. But we share too her growing awareness that her hold on this exalted priest is loosening. She seems ready to contemplate a dallyance with Delio, cut short by the play's gathering pace. She does pick up on a flirtation with Bosola which, from her point of view, looks promising so that she tells him straight 'The only remedy to do me good / Is to kill my longing' (V.2.157–8).

All her men treat her badly. Her husband Castruchio (a neutered character Webster **puns** on 'castrate') neglects her. Her old suitor Delio forgoes any courtesy in his courtship. Bosola, her 'bit of rough', patently is out to use her, calls her foolish when she fails and is happy when she's gone. Her lover Cardinal so despises her openness he poisons her through a kiss. Yet each of them by turn are in her power.

Her lowly place in the story seems a little unfair in its transitoriness. Pescara, the most noble of the nobles, refers to her as 'a strumpet' (V.1.46). She can only be that because sad men have made her so.

CARIOLA

She is a 'foolish woman', a 'superstitious fool'; similar opinions, but at different times, of Bosola and the Duchess. Cast as her mistress's foil, for most of the play Cariola is nevertheless a faithful servant and confidante. For Webster she fulfils the need for a device to impart the Duchess's inner thoughts to the audience without resort to **soliloquy**.

We encounter her first as a hidden witness to her mistress's wooing of her steward. She is clearly out of her depth, nonplussed by the Duchess's apparent impetuosity and unimpressed with the drift and sense of events which she predicts will end unhappily, 'it shows / A fearful madness' (I.2.418–9).

Her's is another role employed by Webster to subtly undermine the integrity and authority of the Catholic Church. But in a different way. Her very orthodox uprightness is perceived as unattractive. As spectators we see little merit in the over-pious prissiness or moralising logic of her disapproval of the Duchess's device to escape her oppressive brothers by a feigned pilgrimage to Loretto. We are inclined to side with her mistress in seeing her objections as superstitious; which is hardly fair, as the pilgrimage to Loretto is Bosola's idea in the first place.

In the event, and in retrospect, it is **ironic** that Cariola's advice might have been wisely followed. Departing from her power-base in Amalfi to travel with an inadequate retinue to hostile and far-away places leaves the Duchess vulnerable to arrest and her ultimate fate.

Cariola's artless beliefs are of little help to her in her end. In fact her integrity collapses in the face of horror. She seems prepared to abandon her scruples and deny her religiosity to avoid death, her psychological collapse all the more stark in comparison with her mistress's fortitude.

We wince to witness this simple maid lie about being pregnant, volunteering to turn informer, claiming to have neglected the obligations of confession and mass (serious sins), resorting to biting and scratching like a cornered cat and ultimately dying by undignified strangulation.

Cariola matches her mistress in the violence of her death, but not in her acceptance of it; the Duchess in control, at peace, her maid at odds with her fate and very much out of control. Yet we have admired her spirit. And there is no reason why we should abandon our approbation because she chooses not to go quietly.

***

For Aristotle character is less important than plot. For Webster interest lies in how character copes with stress, and distress.

Dr Johnson, in the eighteenth century, identified the Shakespearean era as responsible for the development in the theatre of a diversity of individual personality, distinguished from the mode formerly in vogue of a description of type. Johnson's analysis is another way of pinpointing the genesis of a modern phenomenon we know now as '**characterisation**'.

But it is Harold Bloom's insight, in a book published in 1999, *Shakespeare: The Invention of the Human*, which defines a contrast between this 'characterisation', when the substance of the **personae** who people a play is revealed or unfolds, and a concept which somehow organically 'invents the human', when characters develop within a drama and are capable of observable change; and which he refers to as their 'reconceiving' themselves.

One of the questions we must ask, in studying *The Duchess of Malfi*, is whether Bloom's description of this more refined dramatic skill is exclusive to Shakespeare in the Elizabethan and Jacobean period of writing (Bloom's contention), or whether glimpses of it are discernible in the work of other major contemporary craftsmen, Webster amongst them.

NARRATIVE TECHNIQUES & STRUCTURE

This section is closely linked with the later one on Handling of Time and Place. Plays written up to, and including, the Elizabethan era were, more often than not, constructed on an **Aristotelian** model. An Aristotelian pattern demanded consistency with three Unities: Action, Time and Place. From Action there had to be an absence of confusing subplots, Time must portray events taking place within a constricted period, probably no more than a day, and the setting throughout needed to be restricted to one Place. These Unities were considered vital ingredients for a dramatist in his endeavour to maintain audience credibility.

Increasingly, playwrights disregarded this dogma, with Shakespeare and Webster to the fore. Some critics assert that Webster in *The Duchess of Malfi* complies in the main with the strictures imposed by a Unity of Action. They see subplots such as Julia's affair with the Cardinal, events in Loretto and the visit of the deranged to the Duchess as having a bearing on the story. But in a sense all effective subplots add to the main thrust of the drama. An alternative assessment can be made out for a case that suggests that Webster does no more than pay lip service to this Unity.

There can be no question that Webster pays regard to the Unities of Time and Place. A fuller exposition of this is found in the section Handling of Time and Place. Suffice to say here that the action takes place over at least a number of years and is located in, and between, Amalfi, Rome, Loretto and Milan. Webster's contribution to dramatic development was pivotal, in one sense, just because of his flouting of principles accepted as essential up to his time. His abandonment of those conventions, indeed his sometimes displacement of them by an imprecise and vague alternative, adds immensely to a vitality of subversion and therefore to an undermining of certainty, which itself leads to a sustaining of suspense.

Superimposed onto Webster's innovative structure for *The Duchess of Malfi* is a Revenge **Tragedy**, adapted from the **Senecan** model developed by the first century AD Roman philosopher. Intrinsic to such drama is the centrality of language, the inevitability of final disaster, the justifiability of revenge, and the presence of such devices as a play-within-a play, a dumb-show, the menace of the spirit world, displays of madness and masque, and the reporting of off-stage births and deaths. Webster adapts only modestly; he has no ghosts but he does have an echo, the dumb-show is gilded by a commentary from the pilgrims and the deaths are gory and played out on stage.

One of the more subtle structural devices is the way in which Webster has his characters interrelate and there are constant examples of this throughout the play. These contrasts are as unexpected as they are significant:

• Julia, though married, behaves like a prostitute. The Duchess, though single (widowed), is accused by her brothers of having the tendencies of a strumpet. Julia, like the Duchess, does the wooing and dies with dignity. Ironically, Julia's end comes in romantic transit from one corrupt man to another.

- The Duchess reveals at the last a lack of seriousness of faith, contrasting with her maid Cariola's piety, which at her last is linked to a fearful hysteria.
- Within the Aragon family structure are some stark contrasts. One twin is good (The Duchess, though not without blemish) and one evil (Ferdinand, though not without insight). Ferdinand is feverish and passionate, the Cardinal is calculating and cold.
- Two commoners are enticed by ambition; Antonio initially to an uprightness which dissolves into uncertainty, and Bosola to the perfidy of concealment and obscurity.
- The courtiers are either kindly (Pescara) to their sickly colleague (Ferdinand) or display self-indulgence (Castruchio and Malateste).

What is evident in the portrayal of contrasting characters is reflected by the juxtaposition of scenes: For example, Act I ends with Cariola's comment of the madness of her mistress and Antonio's secret marriage and Act II begins with Bosola's judgement of Castruchio's stupidity. The Act ends with Ferdinand's tirade to his brother followed by his self-imposed calm and Act III begins by Antonio informing Delio that Ferdinand's calm is a dangerous and uncharacteristic quietness. And so on. Within the Acts, too, are similar and constant contrasts of mood.

These structural opposites are extended to verbal contrasts. After Ferdinand becomes aware of his sister's sexual activities (because of the obvious evidence of children) he will no longer look upon her. But after her death his 'eyes dazzle' at the sight of her before he departs to 'hunt the badger ... a deed of darkness' (IV.2.328–9). The Cardinal, having arranged his sister's death, knows his secret must be 'a grave dark and obscure' (V.2.268). By contrast, Antonio hears his wife's voice from that grave in an echo as 'a clear light' (V.3.43).

Webster oscillates from structural tightness into vagueness and his contrasts of language and mood are thus sometimes criticised. But there is merit in it; a certain opaqueness is consistent with the playwright's intention to present a reasoned argument which endeavours not to bias. The audience is led from one point of view to its opposite.

Either/or may be frustrating to the simplistic. It is meat and drink to the thoughtful.

STAGING

The first thing to note about staging is that there can be no finally definitive staging. One of the wonders of theatre is that new directors will bring new creative brilliance to a production, which in turn will present the audience with new insights into an old play. The genius of Webster's work is that the drama continues to live and develop after four hundred years.

An examination of the staging of Webster's masterpiece during the period of his active involvement with the theatre must embrace two constituents; the venue of presentation and the cast the playwright had in mind to perform it.

The play is within the general **genre** of Elizabethan Drama, within the same **Senecan** mode developed by Marlowe, Jonson and Shakespeare. It is also Jacobean, with a consequently darker **tone** in an era of restless politics; an unpopular king, an influential censoriousness sourced by the religious fundamentalism of the Puritans, competing with the liberating influences of the **Renaissance** in science, travel and literature. Playwrights, too, are experimenting with comment on a world not necessarily more corrupt than their predecessors, but where rottenness is more evident because of an explosive growth in the power of communication. The Court reacts to this uncomfortably explicit portrayal of its less worthy facets by an increased appetite for the superficiality of entertainments where the critical poignancy of language is less damaging.

The importance, therefore, for Webster of presenting his work in a dedicated theatre is paramount. Not for him the distractions of open spaces and markets, the constriction of churches and the closed environments of the large houses of the nobility, places once in frequent use for the putting on of plays and masques.

The drama was first presented at the private Blackfriars theatre and then at the Globe. The Blackfriars had the advantage over the Globe in that it could be darkened, lighted only by candles; important for the critics who maintain that the whole of the action of *The Duchess of Malfi* took place at night. For such, the intimacy of the Blackfriars would have served such a presentation well. But it was only a third the size of the more public Globe, which had become the resident theatre for The King's Men. They were the leading company of their day and are shown on the title page to be the actors whose services Webster had proudly secured, itself a demonstration that he had by now arrived as a playwright.

The Globe, although built as a theatre, still displayed the design features of an inn courtyard. Around a central pit were ranged galleries which could, sitting and standing, accommodate about two thousand people. A balcony behind the stage was reserved for the kind of innovative presentation Webster sought in the first act where and when Antonio and Delio deliberately perambulate, commentating on the various aspects of the Duchess's court. Such a balcony, too, is an asset in the last act when Bosola violently confronts the Cardinal whose courtiers are outside his chambers above, in anxious conference whether to intervene.

It is difficult from our modern experience of stagecraft, as well as the impact of cinema on drama, to realise how daringly experimental Webster was. But we may get a glimpse of this, four centuries later, when we ourselves are transfixed by a powerful presentation of the play.

HANDLING OF TIME & PLACE

The way the dramatist uses disjointed time as a **metaphor** is examined in the section Imagery and Symbolism. Here we will note Webster's difficulties in the presentation of a story that spans many years in a play which lasts three hours.

Most critics consider that the Duchess, as an historical figure, was about nineteen years of age when the action of the play commences in Act I. At that time she had already borne two children to her first, deceased, husband.

Act II is set at least nine months later. The Old Lady/midwife appears early on in the first scene, and Bosola succeeds in obtaining several indications of the Duchess's advanced pregnancy and ensuing confinement throughout the Act. Webster evidently sees no need to link Acts I and II as the marriage of Antonio and the Duchess at the end of Act I and the Duchess's lying-in in Act II, initiation and **dénouement**, are of a piece.

At the beginning of Act III Antonio tells Delio (and the audience) that there has been yet another lapse of time. Most commentators suggest that this was at least thirteen months, although the calculation does not allow for the possibility of the two further children born being twins; a reasonable conjecture given that the Duchess was one herself. We should note a significant staging opportunity at this point; in the theatre of today, where acts and scenes follow each other quite seamlessly and there is rarely more than one break in a performance, the interval is often suitably taken between Acts II and III.

From the commencement of Act III there are no further major leaps in time, although obviously days will pass as locations move. The passing of time is also indicated by the Cardinal's change of occupation from priest to soldier, though this may have taken place quite swiftly.

The action starts in Amalfi, where it continues up to and including Act II Scene 3. Act II Scenes 4 and 5 are in Rome, returning to Malfi for Act III Scenes 1 and 2, with Scenes 3 and 5 not clearly defined, though probably 'in transit'. Scene 4 is in Loretto. Act IV, in its entirety, is set in Malfi, and most critics suggest that the action for the whole of Act V takes place in Milan, although there is some dispute about that.

Further discussion on Webster's Handling of Time and Place is found in the earlier section Narrative Techniques and Structure and, in particular, the **Aristotelian** concepts of Unity of Time and Place. Suffice to say here that, in regard to the dramatist's handling of time, there are some undeniable problems with a critical opinion that suggests that there is a more or less unbroken flow of action after the beginning of Act III to the end of Act V: For instance, in V.5.107, by which time Antonio's first son has become 'a pretty gentleman', hardly an appropriate description for a play covering a duration beginning a year before his birth and continuing reasonably for a period of two or three years after; although we must note that a short life was predicted in this same son's horoscope in II.3.61.

Time can play tricks on a playwright, too, in remembering detail accurately enough. A famous case in point in relation to this play is the 'right of accession' of the Duchess's son by her first marriage seemingly set aside by Webster at the end of the play. But not only are there other possible explanations to this apparent lapse of consistency; there is also an argument of indisputable simplicity and already touched on elsewhere in this Note which posits that, although memory may be insecure, it is also creative. The loose ends do produce some scintillating theatre.

LANGUAGE & STYLE

We have examined how Webster employed comparisons, contrasts, contradictions and paradoxes in themes, imagery, structure and style. In his characterisations we have seen how family loyalty is flawed and how a servant turned husband becomes a dependant. Some critics maintain that Bosola combines the starkest opposites of light and dark, but about that we would do well to be cautious. His ways are so devious that not even in soliloquy, when theatrical convention dictates that his words to the audience are at their most believable, can we be sure that he is not dissembling with a view to being overheard.

Blank verse is an excellent medium for the playwright's concentrated complexities of plot. Poetry was and is expected to be full of condensed and vivid imagery, and Webster delights in the problems he poses his interpreters in their search for logic and understanding. He seems to approve most of those who conclude that there are no simple answers; that life as he paints it is full of confusion and chaos.

We can have nothing but admiration for a dramatist who breaks with the established conventions of his day to experiment in the creation of such random disharmony. You can study this another way by picking up enigmas in characterisation, of which Bosola, and indeed the Duchess are prime examples.

Substantially, the play is written in the unrhymed iambic pentameter of five stresses and ten syllables per line which was the norm for the blank verse of Renaissance drama. But Webster, like all good playwrights, delighted to bend the rules and some lines are shorter and others longer than the usual pattern. Rhyme is reserved for song and formality, for emphasis, scene closure and moments of jocularity. We can observe the dramatic focus imparted by the following example of a rhyming couplet:

> Go, howl them this: and say I long to bleed.
> *It is some mercy when men kill with speed.* (IV.1.108–9).

Prose provides an opportunity for contrast; for quieter scenes, for depiction of low life, **comedy**, dysfunctioning and derangement, for example IV.2.74–113. Sometimes, Webster heightens the effect of confusion by employing the use of verse for one character and prose for another, both together in the same dialogue (IV.2.114–67). He is also not averse to using the technicalities of language as **metaphor** itself, as by the Duchess to Antonio, 'short syllables / Must stand for time' (III.2.177–8).

By comparable techniques does the dramatist slow down or speed up our perception and anticipation; Antonio and Delio's briefings throughout the play are examples of the former, descriptions of plotting and intrigue, for instance by Julia and Bosola, of the latter.

Webster often uses words to convey a meaning distinct from their literalness. Such **irony** may be so subtle (as opposed to the bluntness of sarcasm) as to be wasted on the audience; and particularly audiences of our current era unused to the nuances in common currency in Jacobean times. When this metaphoric device is evident to the audience but not to the actors it is termed **dramatic irony**, arousing amusement in comic situations and tension in the tragic.

Stylistic convention demanded from serious theatre in Webster's day a play-within-a-play. *The Duchess of Malfi* does not conform to this. It does however incorporate a dumb-show, combined with a commentary on the action by two pilgrims. This artifice of commentary is used by Webster elsewhere in the play in discourse between Antonio and Delio, and in **asides** by an actor on his own to the audience.

We will touch on two other characteristics of style Webster employs to good measure; **metaphor/simile** and distancing. Metaphor (and simile) are discussed elsewhere in connection with Imagery and Symbolism. Poets, like lovers and madmen, are fanciful and can misperceive truth, sometimes wilfully. When the Duchess instructs Antonio to 'Lay a naked sword between us, keep us chaste' (I.2.414) the **innuendo** carries obvious sexual undertones. But she is strong and uses the strong cousin of image, **metaphor**. The **trope** Antonio iterates, in later conversation with the Duchess, is, by contrast, less subtle and less effective. To her fantasy 'the diamonds / Were chang'd to pearls' (III.5.13–14) he responds with a mundane 'the pearls / Do signify your tears' (III.5.16–17). What is really significant is that he can only use a weak (and repeated) **simile** of her much more forceful and original metaphor.

Webster cools (distances) the intensity of his language by at least three stratagems; fables, images of theatre and the Echo. Distancing should perhaps be better described as distracting. The Duchess, in her wooing of Antonio, uses 'St Winifred' almost as a short-hand expletive in response to one of her steward's lines of argument. The point at issue is not the fable of Winifred but that the allusion might distract the audience and decelerate the pace in what is already a very long scene, and with more to go before its climax; we are then led into an investigation of the playwright's intention – to slow down or speed up, to slacken audience tension or to heighten it.

There are other examples of the effectiveness of this contrivance, one of the most poignant being the Duchess's parable of the Salmon and the Dogfish. Her final aphorisms of the scene, 'Men oft are valued high, when th'are most wretch'd … There's no deep valley, but near some great hill' (III.5.140, 143), coming on top of her vivid myth, permit the audience vital relief from the constricting menace of her arrest which immediately precedes. Webster shows, however, that he is a master manipulator of audience psychology by following this deviation with further and fouler menace as Ferdinand plots with Bosola more and insaner torment for his sister.

The theatre as a stylistic totem of 'distancing' is used to great effect again in two instances in Act IV. The Duchess asks Cariola to distract her from the distress of her isolation by recounting 'some dismal tragedy' (IV.2.8). Later in the same scene Webster's contemporary audience will revel in the humour of the actor Richard Burbage's references to himself playing Ferdinand as the Duke damns Bosola's unrelieved villainy 'as we observe in tragedies / That a good actor many times is curs'd / For playing a villain's part' (IV.2.282–4).

A third distancing device Webster uses is the Echo, haunting its way through Act V Scene 3. There is no ghost. Delio does not even believe there is anything present that cannot be explained by natural circumstances. Yet despite the fact that the scene is not without sustained suspense, it does distance the audience temporarily from the horror of Julia's poisoning before tension is awakened once more by the slaying of the servant and the final run of murders.

In the end, language and style are seamless. In Webster's masterpiece they are also unrelenting in the tilt and shift of balance the playwright achieves of disorder in an ordered world. We are swept along in great currents of allusion. There are myths and wild **metaphors** which for all who hear, actors and audience, are close to mental chaos. **Puns** and **irony** and **double entendres** are legion. Logic in dialogue is often abandoned to urgency. To his credit, the writer knows that drama is a far cry from debate.

IMAGERY & SYMBOLISM

In this section we shall concentrate on just a few images to see how the playwright enriches the plot, the characters, but above all the language; how **metaphor** makes the music of the words sing – you can see we are already getting into the swing of it, 'the music of the words'. A lot of fun can be had scanning the text to identify many other images. See how many you can see.

Webster's focus is on the contrast of the world at large with the world of the human condition and, particularly in his case, with forces we can broadly term adverse. It may be cynical but apposite to observe that lawyers (Webster's profession) are primarily concerned with things that go wrong, and how wrongs can be legally righted!

ANIMALS AND BIRDS
These are by far the most frequently mentioned images in the play, and they are generally, but not exclusively, negative. Those listed here are from the first scene; there are many more in the remaining scenes and you will want to look them up and put them into context and category:

Act I
1.38–9   blackbirds   [Bosola]
1.51   crows, pies, caterpillars   [Bosola]

| 1.53 | horse-leech | [Bosola] |
| 1.58 | hawks | [Bosola] |

THE NATURAL WORLD
In a play of such constant tension, nature is more commonly portrayed as harsh or in flux than at ease. The images used to describe such a state have parallels with 'seeming versus reality', 'submerged violence' and 'corruption':

Act I
2.169	thunderbolts	[Bosola]
2.278	wilderness	[Duchess]
2.386–7	time will scatter the tempest	[Duchess]

RANKNESS, CORRUPTION, ANARCHY, DISEASE AND DEATH
These negative attributes from Act I Scene 1 have been listed here but you may wish to investigate each one separately and look for similar examples from the other Acts. The quotes given are by no means exhaustive and you will find many more in this text where some of these **metaphors** are thematic in themselves. Remember that Webster chose to expose moral excesses in high places, escaping any charge of treason by situating his action in a foreign court:

Act I
1.13–15	poison, death, disease	[Antonio]
1.50	standing pools	[Bosola]
1.64	crutches	[Bosola]

VIOLENCE AND MENACE
These are closely associated with the previous group of images. In **Senecan/Renaissance** drama, violent acts frequently take place off-stage. For the playwright, therefore, it is all the more important to portray a convincing anticipation of that violence by extended menace. Here are some examples:

Act III
2.155   earthquakes   [Antonio]
2.156–7 mine, blown-up   [Duchess]
2.321   devil's quilted anvil   [Bosola]

APPEARANCE AND SEEMING CONTRASTED WITH INNER REALITY
Here are a couple of examples but there are a number spread throughout the play:

Act I
2.199   garb of melancholy   [Ferdinand]
2.228   honey-dew ... deadly   [Ferdinand]

OTHER OPPOSITES
The examples listed are representative, not exhaustive:

Act II
3.19   very cold ... yet you sweat [Bosola]
5.77   cold sweat   [Ferdinand]

DISJOINTED TIME
Handling of Time and Place, how the dramatist compresses the events of a number of years into a play which lasts three hours, has already been examined in this Note. A discernible pattern of these time images is how closely allied they are to confusion. Some critics suggest that all the action takes place at night, traditionally a time of unintelligibility.

Disjointed time as a **metaphor** is more opaque than the others we have looked at so far and you will have to search behind the words:

Act III
5.50   hangs upon ... will   [Antonio]

Act IV
1.9   muse four hours   [Bosola]

CONSTRAINTS
Again, there are others:
Act I

| 2.99–101 | law, cobweb, prison | [Delio] |
| 2.243–4 | marriage … prison | [Cardinal] |

GEOMETRY
In contrast to the colour of much of the foregoing, this picture combines
the preciseness you would expect from a scientific image with the strange
tendency to dysfunction, itself a theme of the play:

Act I

| 1.59–65 | slings, swing | [Bosola] |
| 2.57–8 | mathematical, compass | [Ferdinand] |

As has already been indicated, there are positive images to contrast with
the negative, and a number of the former relate to or about the Duchess.
Here, however, is an example from an unexpected source:

Act III

| 2.263 | a cedar, planted by a spring | [Bosola] |

The reader may benefit by comparing this description of Antonio with
Bosola's comments about the Duchess's brothers to Antonio at the
beginning of the play, 'like plum trees, that grow / Crooked over standing
pools' (I.1.49–50), and with Antonio's eulogistic **simile** of the French
king's reforms, 'a Prince's court / Is like a common fountain, whence
should flow / Pure silver-drops in general' (I.1.11–13). This last image
compares, too, with Bosola's agony of tears, after the death of the
Duchess, 'penitent fountains … frozen up' (IV.2.359–60).

You may begin to see how you can use these images in complementary or
contrasting ways to build vivid pictures of themes or characters.

PART FOUR

TEXTUAL ANALYSIS

TEXT 1 (I.2.323–419)

From:

DUCHESS: One of your eyes is bloodshot, use my ring to't,

To:

CARIOLA: A fearful madness: I owe her much of pity.

Antonio returns to Malfi after a long absence in France and meets up with his old friend Delio. They bring each other up to date with events and Antonio observes how corruption pervades the Duchess's court without seeming to taint her. He has an opportunity of acquainting himself with her crooked but princely brothers and their pandering courtiers.

The Duchess sends a message via her maid requesting Antonio to visit her shortly and in the meantime she is canvassed by her brother Ferdinand for the job of stables-master for Bosola, an ex-galley prisoner. Ferdinand would have preferred to recommend Antonio to the Duchess but this idea is vetoed by his older brother the Cardinal. They both wish Bosola to act as their spy on the Duchess's private life, both being intent that their widowed sister should not remarry. They tell her direct of their hostility to marriage in general and hers in particular.

Ferdinand cannot resist a certain coarseness in his conversation with his sister, suggesting that women are drawn to the human organ which most resembles an eel and has no bones. She is understandably outraged, and protests at his indecency. The dissembler deflects her shock by saying that he means the tongue. The Duchess withdraws to her own rooms and confides in her maid Cariola that she has plans of marriage in mind which could prove dangerous. Cariola is to hide behind the arras, to listen and to keep her mistress's confidence.

Antonio enters, assuming he is about to take up his role as steward. He prepares to commit the Duchess's instructions to paper. She speaks to him in gentle terms about her will, and he advises her to remarry and leave all to her new husband. As is to become clear to him later this is indeed her intention. At her prompting he reminisces about his own past and present singleness, his lack of opportunity as yet to marry and have children.

The Duchess presses the ring on Antonio that she vowed never to part with till she remarried (line 323). She says this is a cure for his bloodshot eye. Those in the audience who have seen the play before will reflect that in a later confrontation with Bosola Antonio spontaneously develops a nosebleed. Blood is a ubiquitous theme in the play. Antonio misses the significance of the triviality of the Duchess's suggested cure for his eyesight. The fact is he seems blind (line 328) to her feelings for him. Maybe, she thinks this ring will convince him to see her love better, though he has already encountered two other very different rings; the first with his lance (emblematic of one of the play's sexual subplots) in a riding contest, the winning of which is rewarded by the other, a jewelled gift from Ferdinand (I.2.6–9). Antonio warns of a saucy ambition and the Duchess presses her suit further by placing the ring on his finger. He kneels before her in astonishment.

By the end of the play, the audience will have come to recognise the ring as a symbol of some significance. The Duchess will lose her wedding ring by force to the Cardinal when he relinquishes his (cardinal's ring) at Loretto – his priestly ring of course being a sign of his single-hearted commitment to Christ; perhaps he now feels free to offer a ring of modest protection to his mistress and considers his sister's liaison with Antonio base enough to steal from her. But these constructs are conjecture.

Antonio, meantime, is only too aware that the Duchess is a unique example of widowhood and feminine power. As new steward he cannot afford to be too confident. The Duchess for her part and in her wooing cannot afford to be too obvious. That is why they skirmish. They both know, however, that her act of raising him from his knees (line 336) is a tacit acknowledgement of her counsellor's enhanced social status. Being counsellor to a noble prince inevitably confers preferment.

Antonio is not so foolish as to be unaware of the nuances of what is happening. But he is wary of lunatic ambition. In allowing him to indulge in some homely aphorising Webster may be echoing Montaigne's maxim 'To philosophise is to learn to die'. Certainly the Duchess believes he must now be aware of her intentions, 'now the ground's broke' (line 345). But still he continues to be cautious. Perhaps, he thinks, she alludes, in making him lord of her mine (line 346), to his role as chamberlain of her household; a nice **pun** when what she really intends is to make him 'mine'. He declaims his unworthiness. She persists, defining him as her ideal man (line 352). The **irony** will be that he will turn out to be very far from that – a seriously flawed though honest fellow of modest ability. So he promotes that honesty (in this instance probably inferring his chastity) which, he says, has been to date a one-sided transaction he has never drawn upon; which she therefore promptly now invites him to do.

She rues she has to lead the wooing (line 358). In choosing as husband an upwardly mobile steward who is not vain, she has run the risk of someone who is mediocre. She insists she looks for a 'complete man'. She wants this man to 'awake' (line 371), and soon. She wills him to stir himself, to bridge the antinomy of servant and governor; he is her steward and must become lord of her wealthy mine.

The Duchess reminds Antonio she is a young widow (line 373), a phrase which she admits brings her only half a blush. Ferdinand has already called her lusty, attributing to that epithet the implication of sin. Antonio sees sin in terms of ambition, a characteristic he eschews. He does admit, though, to a desire for pure and honourable love. He offers her his protection. She offers him her love, employing a stewardly **metaphor**, that of balancing the books of account, any debts, actual or metaphoric, being cancelled. (Later on, stewardly misfeasance will be the public reason for his dismissal.). She kisses him. Still his caution is alert. What about your brothers (line 383), he enquires?

But she is now impatient, and aroused. In her heat she is unconscious she is entering the essence of **tragedy**, whose elements of fear and pity she contrasts. The attitude of her brothers, she insists, is to be pitied, not feared. Time will heal the rift – an axiom of hope Antonio anxiously carries with him when he seeks restitution with her brothers in Act V. For now, he approves her forthrightness which he recognises he should share but does not, 'These words should be mine' (line 387). Perhaps too, he already recognises what the audience will, too, before long; that by status and even more by temperament she is the stronger and assumes a role that in a more equal marriage should be his.

The pace of the scene has become frenetic. She cannot wait. The language Webster uses betrays that. Sentences are short, instructions come staccato. 'Kneel', she says; a command to them both – interrupted by the ineptly inappropriate appearance of Cariola. This is an entrance beloved of dramatists; an unexpected intrusion into a delicate moment. It happens at other times in the play, notably when Bosola appears after Julia's murder.

Cariola enters. She is the Duchess's counsellor, too, who now becomes concealer of her secret. Secrecy is the downside of counselling. And paradoxically, taking the law into your own hands, which is what the Duchess now does, is the beginning of a loss of power. But she is happy to see her power diluted if that means sharing it with Antonio; indeed she has a mind to 'put off all vain ceremony' (line 372). One of the most persistent criticisms levelled at the Duchess is that she puts personal pleasure before her responsibilities of state.

Now she propels them both into a ceremony which, she says, makes their marriage absolute. There is, though, a cloud of violence on her horizon. Perhaps this cloud occurs because there has been a reversal of values in Malfi: Her secret and permanent contract with Antonio can be dismissed out of hand by one brother, Ferdinand, whilst by contrast the other, the Cardinal, lives openly in an irregular, adulterous and casual relationship with his mistress.

The Duchess and Antonio make their vows in romantic mood. The audience will be aware that such a marriage is given full recognition in English law. But now it is she who hesitates, is anxious, wondering if the Church will be satisfied to accept their absolute marriage. Her paranoia is reasonable in the scale of early-seventeenth-century sensibilities. The Church is powerful and can 'force' (line 401) whatever it wills. Church and State are massively intertwined. The Cardinal was a soldier before, and will become a soldier again. The Pope has a powerful army and easy access to the discreet resources of the Holy Roman Emperor. In Webster's England the situation is intensified – the sovereign is also head of the Church.

Antonio's response is to reaffirm his wish, declared earlier (lines 304–14), for a marriage located in heaven. The Duchess is not much reassured by platitudes. Is there any way that the Church can say it could have bound together better? And by implication unbind it easier? In other words, can the Church interfere? The cruel **irony** is of course that the Church will interfere to try and discredit their marriage. The Church is not, in fact, interested in binding their marriage, but in destroying it. She must reassure herself as well as Antonio, 'We now are man and wife' (line 405), and insist that the Church can only echo that. Again the sad irony is that the Church's echo is absent when Antonio hears the echo of his dead wife's voice predict 'Thou art a dead thing' (V.3.38).

But now the Duchess has grown hot again and wills her man to sweep her off to bed. Aware she may frighten her coy new husband with her forward zeal, she titillates that they are only off to plot about what she calls with irony and optimism her 'humorous' (line 412) brothers. Playfully she suggests 'a naked sword' (line 414) be laid between them to keep them chaste, the last thing on her mind. Thomas Lacqeur, a late-twentieth-century critic, observes that it was only 'sometime in the late eighteenth century [that] the old belief that women needed to experience orgasm in order to conceive was abandoned'. For Webster, therefore, woman's passion had not yet degenerated into passivity. Hence the plot's need for her need to almost simultaneously wed and bed. It was quite common for women not to marry until pregnant, and other recent critics have suggested that women in the process of producing and rearing children could be so obsessed with that activity as to be considered mad. In such circumstances, akin to madness, it was a husband's duty to protect his vulnerable wife from outside harm. Alluding to the old fable of Alexander and Lodowick (see the footnote in the New Mermaids edition) only serves to increase the frisson she conjures up; the fact that the men in the myth were probably twins serves to sharpen the focus of contrast between her twin, Ferdinand, and her husband Antonio.

Love and madness come inexorably to be seen as indissoluble. That, at any rate is Cariola's judgement. The two she watches hurry off to bed may be locked in greatness, but it is a greatness of madness which combines fear and pity, and therefore augurs **tragedy**. It is however a tragedy delayed. In the second Act, about to commence, the fruits of the Duchess's Edenic marriage are soon revealed, a disclosure brought on through greed for early apricots, offered by Bosola in the guise of charming human serpent.

The audience have witnessed a display of counsel and courtship. Now confinement and corruption are lurking at the door.

TEXT 2 (III.1.36–III.2.35)

From:

ANTONIO: Of love, or marriage, between her and me,

To:

CARIOLA: In three several young men, which should I choose?

Some years have elapsed since the start of the play. The Duchess has had three children by Antonio. Bosola has had proof (by mislaid horoscope) of the first which he passed on to his mentors. This 'intelligence' drives Ferdinand into paroxysms of sexual jealousy, and prompts another fact-finding visit to his sister in Malfi. Antonio naively believes the secret of the Duchess's growing family is concealed from her brothers.

Ferdinand arrives and, on a pretext of tiredness, announces his imminent progress to bed. But before he goes he cannot resist taunting his sister about plans he has of a husband for her. He is in a dangerously **oleaginous** mood, however, being transparently insincere about Malateste ('great'), Antonio ('worthy') and the Duchess (referring to her 'innocency'). We know he means not a word of what he actually says from the conversation he is about to have with Bosola. Meanwhile, his sister ridicules his suggestion of marriage to Malateste on two counts, both of which will engage the audience by their **irony**. The man proposed is a 'mere stick of sugar-candy' (line 42). The attributes suggested combine those of sugar-daddy and the opaque clarity of crystal. Malateste is hollow, superficial and, possibly as a **pun** on his name implies ('bad seed'), sexually inadequate. Antonio, whom she has covertly married, is by no means as deficient as that, but the audience will have begun to become uneasy about his intrinsic strength. That the Duchess prefers to be dominant will be a view they are beginning to formulate.

She dismisses her brother's mild suggestion as well because of Malateste's low-born pedigree. A count, she mocks? I am a Duchess. I can do better for you than that. In terms of class she has in fact already done worse. She has married a commoner, but she has indeed done better by character than a Malateste; confirmed by Ferdinand's prescient confidence, 'You shall do well in't' (line 45). Immediately he switches his focus to Antonio, a conjoining of remarks too close for comfort, almost too close to be coincidence. His attention directed at her husband is swiftly and skilfully marginalised, however, by the Duchess's introduction of a different issue which she deems best now to confront head-on.

No doubt her Malfi rabble's opinion of her as 'a strumpet' (III.1.26) has been the subject of pillow talk between her and Antonio. No doubt her brother will have heard or will hear the rumour too. Ferdinand, however, is not ready yet for nastiness. He soothes her by sympathising with her being the subject of idle talk to which, he says, even if there were substance he would excuse. Going, he leaves his sting, 'be safe / In your own innocency' (lines 54–5). He simulates a priestly role. His Christianity is essentially misogynist. Women, this woman, are/is innately sinful.

Out of earshot of all except Bosola, Ferdinand fulminates on the Duchess's guilt which his intelligencer confirms, without hard evidence of who it is that has fathered her three bastards. He prefaces his talk of her children by appearing to report a rumour (line 59). This prevarication is his skilful way of introducing the issue; he cannot be that detached from the goings on of the household not to be aware of the increasing number of children around. But he is being cautious. Ferdinand is a volatile person. Nevertheless, Bosola is sure that the father is 'desertless' (line 65) or she would not be ashamed to acknowledge him. This secrecy is her significant undoing. Ferdinand wonders out loud if a person can be made to fall in love involuntarily. Bosola thinks so, but the Duke rejects such as superstition, whilst admitting that aphrodisiacs can induce a kind of love close to madness.

Again the Duke is moved to angry thinking of his sister. There is a seductive slippage in his speech from generalities to the particular; from the cunning of sorcerers and mountebanks to an accusation that she is a witch, which carries a not-so-veiled capital threat. Admittedly he is not so keen at first at the suggestion made by Bosola of the Duchess being a sorcerer. He soon, however, seems to embrace the idea as if it was his own; it allows him a sound reason for distancing himself from her. The witchcraft he despises 'in her rank blood' (line 78) is another **irony** in view of their filial relationship. He is impatient to make her confess. The discourse between the Duke and his intelligencer thus takes on the nature of subliminal violence, simulated by the playwright in staccato interjections, a language of **onomatopoeia**: 'a false key / Into her bed-chamber' 'I have' 'As I would wish' 'What do you intend to do?' 'Can you guess?' 'No' 'Do not ask then' (lines 80–3) and so on. Ferdinand finds Bosola surly if not actively obstructive. The Duke enjoys the penumbra of obscurity in which he moves. Bosola sees this as an affectation. Ferdinand, he thinks, is much too taken up in the belief of his own publicity; so that now, in the absence of other flatterers surrounding him, he must flatter himself. Once again, the Duke uses a soft answer. Yes, he says, my company has been usually amongst flatterers until I met you, Bosola. I appreciate your friendship in telling me so straightforwardly of my shortcomings, and this will prevent my ruin.

Bosola is not accustomed to hearing anyone call him friend.

Webster, master-craftsman of startling contrast, follows this menace with a scene of great mellifluousness, at least at its beginning. Antonio is no match for the Duchess's teasing. She means to make him earn her favours 'with cap and knee' (line 5). Removing the cap and bending the knee is what gentlemen do naturally to those of higher status. The status of women, however, particularly married women, is so overshadowed by their husbands that she suggests, in a line of intimate **rhetoric**, sleeping together should attract a fee. Her humour meets with a peevish response from Antonio; I must, he iterates, I must. Must, she retorts, 'you are a lord of mis-rule' (line 7). Mis-rule and madness go together. Cariola deduced as much and termed it 'fearful madness' (I.2.419) when first this couple made their secret vows and hurried off to bed.

Antonio slips inadvertently into the **pun** and claims his nightly governance, to which the Duchess responds by playing along with a subservient role 'To what use will you put me?' (line 9).

At this point in the bantering encounter between the Duchess and Antonio we are able to observe the androgyny of them both which works at a social, political and personal level. She is ruler, aristocrat, quick-witted, a natural leader; but she is woman, wife, and mother. He is counsellor, commoner, studied, by inclination student rather than teacher; he is also a man, superior, father. But being too certain about cross-gendering is a dangerous pastime, particularly with Webster. This pair do not encourage neat categorising and as audience we are left to ponder what exactly is the playwright's subversive radical but discreet agenda.

When she mocks the euphemism of 'sleep', the implication of lust in such spicy talk becomes too much for Cariola's continued silence. The maid's **innuendo** carries more wit than Antonio's laboured wisdom. Once more he is ponderous in his response to her **double entendre** 'Wherefore still, when you lie with my lady / Do you rise so early?' (lines 17–18). Again, the Duchess displays a hot impetuosity by kissing him. He demands another kiss, which he initiates himself.

From which he launches into a discourse on marriage. He queries Cariola's aspirations on the matter. Her negative response is **ironic** when set beside her execution protestations later, 'I am contracted / To a young gentleman' (IV.2.243–4), and 'I am quick with child' (IV.2.249). But for now her apparent shrewishness prompts Antonio to a disapprobation of singleness, using examples from classical mythology to point up the fruitlessness, the emptiness, the coldness of eschewing matrimony, compared with the lush flowering, the value added, the shining brightness of those 'transhap'd' 'by a gracious influence' (line 30), by implication, by marriage.

All this seems somewhat simplistic, and its superficiality is soon to be demonstrated by events, when Antonio's idyll with the Duchess is to be disrupted for ever. Cariola finds their foreplay too poetic, and taunts Antonio with some real philosophy; what should she go for, wisdom, riches or beauty? Antonio is out of his depth and can only trivialise such a question. It is too difficult, he admits, which naked and amorous woman to choose for a man who is blind. Whilst the discussion continues, and the Duchess muses into her mirror, and the audience begins to anticipate a scene of sensuality developing, Webster removes Antonio from the stage, busy with Cariola devising a game of hide-and-seek. Alone, but unaware of it, the Duchess indulges in apostrophic **innuendo**. The **dramatic irony** is that she is not alone for long enough for her secret to remain safely intact.

TEXT 2 continued

It is Antonio and Cariola's juvenility which opens the door to Ferdinand's inhumanity and precipitates the Duchess's undoing.

TEXT 3   (V.2.264–343)

From:

CARDINAL: By my appointment the great Duchess of Malfi

To:

BOSOLA: That throws men down, only to raise them up.   *Exit.*

Things have fallen apart. For everyone. That is the nature of **tragedy**.

We need little more introduction to this passage than the Cardinal gives us in his first three lines. The Duchess and her family escape from Malfi, only to be banished from Ancona and Loretto. Antonio escapes to Milan with their oldest son. As soon as he leaves her, she and the two younger children are arrested by Bosola, taken back to Malfi, tortured and strangled. Bosola continues to be the reluctant spy of the Aragon brothers, although the younger Ferdinand now becomes clinically insane. Julia confesses to Bosola her infatuation for him and he decides to use this to find out what is troubling the Cardinal, and whether his rating with the Emperor is on the wax or wane. She interrogates her former lover so persistently as to what might be his problem that he yields to her, warning however that her knowledge will hurry her to ruin (line 254).

Julia's outburst of horror at the Cardinal's statement about the demise of his sister and her children (and his hand in it) is not so much at the murder as at his confession. She does herself no service in admitting she has betrayed him. Indeed, she has not betrayed him. He has let out his own secret.

This play is much about secrets and his is now revealed, and not just to her. But as yet he doesn't know why she says he is undone. His conscience is as much at sleep as his intelligence. He only knows he must fulfil his prophecy that it would have been better for her not to know. So he enters into his blasphemy, referring dismissively to the Bible as 'this book', poisoning its outside the inside of which has already condemned him, and making her kiss, most religiously, its deadly cover.

Bosola's timing is not often awry and we have little reason to believe it has failed him now. He emerges from hiding, to find Julia dying and himself discredited. Ever the opportunist, he is only disappointed with Julia for not turning the poisoned Bible back upon her lover. He turns her death, however, into a convenient moment to remind the Cardinal of an account overdue for 'service' rendered.

The Cardinal, thoroughly discountenanced, loses his composure for the first time. Not that he will do anything himself. 'I'll have thee hew'd in pieces' (line 287). He always has other people to do his dirty work for him. But Bosola is used to being treated rough and knows he is in a commanding position; he is privy to the Cardinal's latest murder and is not about to allow him to gain the upper hand. In fact he trades insult with insult, suggesting that where recently there has been treason afoot the Cardinal is at work again, hiding himself where the former conspirators did, vaulted well below ground. 'Fair marble' (line 292), of course, is the colour for tombstones, **oxymoronic** when set beside 'rotten purposes' (line 293) and **ironic** from the mouth of Bosola.

Webster invests Bosola with the sense of being an actor both here and at the end of the play and in doing so shares with them the same professional rootlessness, being misunderstood as a chameleon. But Webster implies much more than this. A few years earlier one of the most momentous incidents in the early reign of James I took place. On 5 November 1605 Guy Fawkes, a converted catholic, attempted to blow up the houses of parliament with king and members present. He was caught red-handed, with his kegs of gunpowder intact, in the crypt of the Palace of Westminster, traditional burying place for the famous. His treason failed and he was executed in January 1606. Clearly, it seems possible that the playwright, in Bosola's accusation, has this incident in mind, but of course he cloaks it as a **metaphor** for the happenings in the Duchess's Italy:

> Unless you imitate some that do plot great treasons,
> And when they have done, go hide themselves i'th' graves
> Of those were actors in't (lines 294–6).

But there is still something more going on here. We simply do not know enough about the complex life of William Cecil, first Lord Burghley, and Queen Elizabeth's chief minister from early in her reign until his death in 1598. In politics and religion he owed his staying power to a certain dextrous pragmatism. It is likely that Christopher Marlowe (a man from humble background 'improved' by immense scholarship) was one of a number of 'intelligencers' he employed to spy on plotting Catholics until his untimely death in 1593. In the quotation above, 'some that do plot great treasons', Webster may have had Cecil, Marlowe or Walsingham (or someone of equivalent stature) in mind; although all three men were pro-Elizabeth and pro-Protestant, some of the plots of the period were quite bizarre enough for the instigators being highly connected double-agents to be a credible possibility.

Bosola presses home his advantage, drawing on that learning portrayed with such profligacy throughout the play, learning that Delio refers to him with disdain, 'I knew him in Padua, a fantastical scholar' (III.3.40). What Bosola does, with a display of flashing brilliance, is to turn the ordinary words 'fortune' and 'honour', which bear positive connotations and by which the Cardinal attempts to seduce him to look forward to a brighter future, into their classical **tropes**. So that 'Fortune' for Bosola is a Greek goddess from whom he may derive poverty as well as riches, pain as well as blessing, misfortunes as well as pleasure; whereas 'Honour', a Roman equivalent, has never been a verity he has aspired too. 'There are a many ways that conduct to seeming / Honour, and some of them very dirty ones' (lines 300–1).

The Cardinal is tired of philosophising and tired of Bosola, who he now will use to help him hide the results of his own dirty work, and then dispose of him. The Cardinal now thinks of Julia as 'that body' (line 306). As audience we know he has only ever thought of Julia in that way. He wants to lull Bosola towards the death of Antonio, 'kill' being an anodyne euphemism for what in truth will be another 'murther' (lines 305, 309). The Cardinal would like to make sure Bosola follows instructions by pressing upon him a substantial force. Bosola is aware the Cardinal wants him compromised, but wants no such encumbrance around to implicate him. He makes his point by base images, and Webster has him stray, for strong effect, into **prose**.

The Cardinal is plainly not quite back to his sanguine self and shows anxiety in Bosola's return. 'Come to me after midnight' (line 315) is followed by 'Fail not to come' (line 322). Of course he doesn't want Julia's body on his hands. He is also anxious to have Antonio's demise confirmed. Only then, can he rid himself of Bosola.

The Cardinal's departure is signalled by a sexual **innuendo**, 'by that you may conceive / What trust I plant in you' (lines 323–4). The **irony** is that neither of the men on stage is fit for any conceiving and neither is capable of planting, giving or receiving trust. One has just killed his former mistress; the other had been contemplating taking her on as his wanton, but on sober reflection is happy he does not have to do so. Bosola tells the Cardinal that Julia's removal has done him 'a very happy turn' (line 321); although it is possible that Bosola is here hinting at Castruchio's absence – one less troublesome body to remove.

Bosola is left on stage to **soliloquise** as he did at the end of Act IV following the death of the Duchess. Two women he professed to love have been murdered. He has expressed remorse before, 'we cannot be suffer'd / To do good when we have a mind to it' (IV.2.353–4). He does so again, but this time tinged with a new note of sincerity in his repentance. 'O penitence, let me truly taste thy cup' (line 342). But we are dealing with a neglected and rejected figure whose only hope of consolation is for a better status. So he cannot resist adding, 'That throws men down, only to raise them up' (line 343).

Bosola knows he must move carefully, suspects a Cardinal who 'bears up' (line 331) well when wallowing in blood and who has plans which are only short-term for the likes of him. The intelligencer has no intention now of breaking his neck. Meanwhile we witness the emergence of a new attribute, pity. The cruel **irony** for 'good Antonio' (line 333) is that the safety Bosola wills for him is not going to be in the hands of Bosola, who indulges in a contemplation of an **oxymoronic** 'just revenge' (line 338). In Jacobean drama, with revenge goes the inevitability of **tragedy**. As we have seen in our study of Revenge (see Recurring Themes), taking the law into one's own hands may have been morally defensible in the recent **Renaissance** past, but with a more regularised and codified system of justice, it is no longer legal. Revenge may be a personal response to a perceived wrong. It cannot be considered just.

But Bosola has never been concerned with the finesse of law. He has acted on commission. The Duchess's echo (Act V Scene 3),when she haunts her husband's imagination, comes to haunt her servant first. Bosola dismisses it. It is the melancholy of the **malcontent**, a madness very far removed from his hopeless hope of being raised.

PART FIVE

Background

John Webster

His life

We know even less about the life of Webster than we do about Shakespeare. It appears that he was born c. 1578–9, the oldest son of a coachmaker whose business was in Cow Lane, situated in London's Smithfield and within the parish of St Sepulcre. His father was a member of the Merchant Taylor's Company, which Webster himself claims to be a freeman of in 1623. Young John probably attended the Company school before being admitted to the New Inn of the Middle Temple in 1598.

As we know little about Webster's life, so we know little about his death. The year was probably 1634. But this very sparseness of information about one of the foremost Jacobean playwrights can be a benefit. It prevents our being distracted by his circumstances from the drama. Or rather, it stops us from confusing images which come to us by courtesy of his genius with impressions garnered from his biography. We are freed from the person to appreciate the work, and in an uncluttered way.

Of course this introduces a paradox. Most modern critics are very concerned about contextuality. Because we know so little about the man, we are driven to concentrate on textuality, on his writing. In an almost uncanny way this should lead us on to meeting and knowing the writer and his thinking more intimately and more exactly.

His dramatic work

As well as having an evident taste for and experience of the theatre, Webster's plays betray the broad range of his reading and are strewn with references to his training and profession as a lawyer.

In the early 1600s he appears to have collaborated with other playwrights in a number of theatrical ventures, the texts of which are now lost.

The first play he wrote alone was not initially well received. *The White Devil* (1612) experiments with some of the ideas and themes later reworked in the more immediately popular play under consideration in this Note. Both are set at court, both invoke ghosts, both focus on a heroine and both are tragedies.

The Duchess of Malfi (1614) also, like Webster's preceding play, features a **malcontent**. Both men become aware of the birth of pity within themselves, but Bosola's remorse and his response to it affect the final outcome of the play in a manner not available to Flamineo. In the fourth act, too, the Duchess becomes so intensely the focus that the dramatic nature of her unfolding torture surpasses anything realised in Webster's former work. It became common in this era of drama (and often persists to our own day) to define a person by their position or role in society; so that the Duchess's assertion of her identity takes on a political as well as a personal significance. The fact that her last words to her maid are maternal instructions gives substance to the view of Webster's politically liberal, even matriarchal sensibility.

Although Webster was only 33 when the play was first performed, it was nearly another ten years before it was published. There were certain intrinsic dangers in the printing of such a play; not only the neurotic censorship rife at the time but also the danger of text piracy.

The last play Webster is known to have written by himself is *The Devil's Law Case* (1616). The audience is encouraged to think this is going to be another **tragedy**, but it ends in **comedy**, both in the classical and colloquial sense. Webster continued to maintain his interest in the sort of fraught political events well known to his spectators and, like the other plays, there is a constant tension of gender, with women cast in the tragic role.

Not much is known of the rest of Webster's theatrically productive life, or indeed any other part of it. This forces a benefit on the reader, to concentrate on his texts. He is thought to have worked with Rowley on *A Cure for a Cuckold*. Rowley, like Shakespeare, was a journeyman actor. Tragicomedy suited his experience in the theatre. It suited Webster's wide reading and lawyerly ambiguity as well. He shies away from the simplistic, he is almost always for and against, increasing confusion in or out of justice. He feels for the absurd within the abject and the sad within the glad, attributes we see in all his work and not least in *The Duchess of Malfi*.

WEBSTER & THE ENGLISH RENAISSANCE

It would be wrong to think that nothing was happening in the Dark Ages. The western world was in winter, where much was happening though mostly unseen. Europe was saving itself for the tremendous burst of energy about to be outpoured.

The **Renaissance** (how this movement came to be known in the nineteenth century) was a reawakening of interest and discovery in science and the arts, carried along by an explosion of learning and enquiry and spearheaded by the universities; in short, a curiosity about everything, coupled with a willingness to challenge orthodoxy. Genesis for this 'rebirth' can be attributed to the Italy of the twelfth century, although inspiration for it was drawn from such earlier influences as the inventiveness of the Moors and the sophistication of the Byzantine civilisation.

Literature, of course, as a branch of scholarship, was active in this progress, aided by an increasing literacy and an advancing technology in the art of reproduction, particularly printing. Drama, as a branch of literature, unshackled from the more traditional label of elitism attached to **genres** like poetry, was freed to be a vehicle at the vanguard of the new thinking. The theatre of representation and type made way for the theatre of individualism. A symptom of that gradual transition is a move away from poetry towards **prose**; the poetic coarsened by the prosaic.

The impetus the Renaissance brought to England was just as forceful as elsewhere, if necessarily delayed by Britain's geographical isolation on the edge of Europe. A steady influx of Italians into England in the Elizabethan period encouraged the forces of change, and writers such as Marlowe, Jonson, Webster and Shakespeare found that drama was a genre where their innovative intelligence was encouraged to flourish by concentrating on coherent themes and narrative plots.

At the same time a generalised morality in dramatic themes was giving way to a more converged realism, which in the Jacobean era became increasingly more focused and sombre. Webster would have been aware, however, of the ever-present risk of intrusion by the censor; Phillip of Spain's heir had been strangled in prison and madness was hereditary in the royal blood. Political suspicion could thus be neatly side-stepped by setting plays in Italy and Spain.

The new breed of playwright, which of course included Webster, also found that using a cultured but Italian venue for their plots provided a safe (because foreign) landscape for the exploration of ideas and the expression of opinions which would have been politically unacceptable, even dangerous, if a 'home' setting had been employed. We do well to remember that the first public performance of *The Duchess of Malfi* came only nine years after Guy Fawkes narrowly failed to blow up King and Parliament in the Gunpowder Plot. A substantial Catholic minority was still determined to restore a Catholic monarch and return religious authority to Rome, and a powerful Protestant Puritanism was equally determined to prevent this.

Renaissance literature really came of age in the golden period of creativity bound at its start by the maturing Elizabethan statement, the heralding of Sidney's *An Apology for Poetry* in 1580, and culminating at the end of the Jacobean reign of James I. One of the significant reasons why present day readers find such drama 'difficult' is because writers like Webster and his contemporaries were rediscovering the potency of the ancient texts of Rome and Greece. Paradoxically, this emphasis on the Classical past was progressive, highlighting as it did the place of reason and logic and going hand in hand with radical discoveries in a diverse range of learning; the revolutionary science of Galileo, the restless wanderings of Columbus, the reforming religious zeal of Luther, and the liberal philosophies of Machiavelli, Montaigne and Bacon, to cite just some of the more noteworthy examples.

Webster's thinking, reflected in his plays, is very much a product of this experimental age of ferment. We have no clear indication of his personal beliefs, or indeed whether he believed anything at all. But he wrote in a spirit of enquiry, his characters challenging the status quo of the establishment and undermining accepted values. His attitude does not imply, however, that he was an anarchist. Although his plots travel through unharmonious and disruptive situations, there always emerges before the final curtain a certain kind of order. To end otherwise would have been neither artistically consonant with accepted form or personally safe. But State and religious authority is definitely the loser in *The Duchess of Malfi*, being **parodied** as cunning corruption; the Cardinal is exposed as a moral hypocrite and his ducal brother goes mad. Their wayward but noble sister is revealed as heroic in her powerlessness. And Bosola, the servant of all three, is shown to be amoral whilst endowed by the playwright with an acute perception – we are encouraged to reject him but embrace his insights. In short, good order as a code for living is almost an intrinsic raison d'être during the English Renaissance; hence in the play the Duchess's brothers' anguish at her behaviour and her husband Antonio's anxiety at its potential exposure.

The period witnessed and gave rise to a great upsurge within two institutions, national identity and religious individualism. Webster's Italian setting would have been tacitly understood by his audience as a distancing device. But equally, the situations he devised would have been recognised, through their disguise, as apposite to an English application; effeminate courtiers, corrupt princes, sycophantic servants and compromised priests. Religion was as much a burning issue (almost literally) in England as Italy. The Pope had excommunicated the Tudor monarchs and relieved English Catholics of allegiance to the English Crown. So from 1558 (when the Virgin Queen ascended the throne) and onwards English Catholics were seen as actually disloyal and potentially traitors. Even Queen Elizabeth's relative, Mary Queen of Scots was, as a devout Catholic, suspected of treason and thus executed in 1587. Underlying Webster's play is a Protestant sentiment of contempt for authority in the practice of religion; the Duchess marries again when told not to do so, she marries a commoner, she marries in secret. And we never see her in church, except at Loretto, where she is subjected to the abuse of Church injustice and State exile. Working against these sympathies is the strong Protestant approval of a female ruler (modelled on Queen Elizabeth) who eschewed marriage for the good of her people. In our own day liberal-minded people associate themselves with enlightened tolerance. Thus Webster assumes iconic status and we can associate our views with those he seems to be sympathetic towards; and they encompassed a wide range of opinion.

READING WEBSTER

Most critics agree that the authoritative extant texts of *The Duchess of Malfi* are more for the benefit of readers than performers. Evidence for this is in the many instances in the first quarto, the production of which was carefully overseen by the author, of italics and quotation marks. Obviously such marks are of little pertinence to a cast of journeymen actors.

Sometimes the text adopts an idiosyncratic rhythm which presents the unwary reader with some confusion. This happens, for instance, where a complete line of **iambic pentameter** is split into two or more speeches. A line or more of verse is thus saved, or perhaps it is extended. Examples of this practice appear throughout the play and here we will highlight just two:

BOSOLA: Must I see her again?

FERDINAND: Yes.

BOSOLA: Never.

FERDINAND: You must.

BOSOLA: Never in mine own shape;

(IV.1.130–1)

CARIOLA: If you kill me now
I am damn'd. I have not been at confession
This two years.

BOSOLA: When!

CARIOLA: I am quick with child.

BOSOLA: Why then,
Your credit's sav'd: bear her into th' next room.

(IV.2.247–50)

With practice the student will find reading the play an exhilarating experience. The secret is to read it for the first time like you do a novel, as fast as is coherently possible. It will take you two or three hours. Miss out the notes, the introductory pages, the difficult words. You will then find you have at least a chance of matching Webster's vigour and pace of action, and his impact of varied language. Afterwards, read it again, ` slowly, like you would any text you are mining for meaning.

PART SIX

C RITICAL HISTORY &
BROADER PERSPECTIVES

Broadly, there are two kinds of critical comment valid for Webster's drama; that which applies to the play text and that which applies to stage performance. Sometimes it is impossible to isolate the one from the other. In the paragraphs which follow, we will trace a history of criticism which will often mingle, consciously or unconsciously, the two strands.

For convenience and simplicity we will divide this critical history by century. The epithets we may attach to each can only be approximately appropriate, but nevertheless help to offer a flavour of the type of writing and type of criticism to be found in that era. A section of criticism contemporary with our own era is finally appended.

S EVENTEENTH-CENTURY CRITICISM – RENAISSANCE

F.L. Lucas, in his authoritative four-volume survey of the life and works of Webster (1927), draws an apt analogy between the poet and his Duchess, who both seem to him to sit 'bayed about with madmen'.

Part of the reason Webster did not gain a prominence in his own time to rival Marlowe and Jonson was that his detractors did not understand what he was setting out to do. He was attempting to deliver scenes of great theatre, suffused with fine poetry. But he was doing it at a time and in an atmosphere that attached no great importance to drama as literature. Whilst being a son of the **Renaissance**, there is a sense in which he challenged the utilitarian rationalism that emerged hand in hand with **humanism**.

Nevertheless, Webster did receive bouquets from his contemporaries for his play and we have to start looking for these no further than the first original edition. Middleton, in rhyming couplets of dubious merit, asserts that his 'monument is rais'd in thy life time' and calls it a 'masterpiece of tragedy'. Rowley's verse is not much more distinguished but his view of *The Duchess* is equally generous, 'Yet my opinion is, she might speak more; / But never (in her life) so well before'. And Ford, in the same introductory pages to *The Duchess of Malfi*, proclaims 'Crown him a poet, whom nor Rome nor Greece, / Transcend in all theirs, for a masterpiece'.

Not all Webster's contemporaries are complimentary, however. Henry Fitzjeffrey finds his workmanship laborious and the Venetian envoy, Orazio Busino, objected to his play on religious grounds.

Pepys, in his *Diary* on 2 November 1666, reports reading *The Duchess* whilst travelling, 'which seems a good play'. A week later he refers to it as 'pretty good'. Three weeks later he has obviously thought again and terms it a 'sorry play'. From this time on the play's reputation declined, despite (perhaps partly because of) adaptations by producers to conjure up more catchy titles, and 'borrowings' by other playwrights of plot and themes.

EIGHTEENTH-CENTURY CRITICISM – AUGUSTAN

Webster's work was now in for a century of neglect. In 1728, Pope makes a passing reference to Webster as one of a number of 'tolerable writers'. Again, there were a number of adaptations, notably by Nahum Tate and Lewis Theobald, whose plagiarisms demeaned the original into disrepute and farce. The latter heaped insult on injury by accusing Webster of being a 'wild and undigested genius' and it was John Webster whose standing suffered when Theobald's poor copy 'met with the Fate it deserved', according to an anonymous reviewer in the Grubstreet Journal.

NINETEENTH-CENTURY CRITICISM – ROMANTIC

This period ushered in a new breed of critic, foremost of whom was Charles Lamb. The mode of criticism became more romantic than analytic, more impressionistic than investigative. Basically, Lamb was enthusiastic about Webster and this spilled over into other commentators. John Wilson is appreciative of this 'master of scenes' but critical of his structures and examines the problems of having the main character die in the fourth of a five act play. Hazlitt's opinion is that *The*

Duchess comes 'the nearest to Shakespear of any thing we have upon record', although the final grizzly scenes 'exceed the just bounds' of **tragedy**. Sir Walter Scott, in a letter in 1831 to Rev Alexander Dyce, acclaims Webster as 'one of the best of our ancient dramatists'.

For the remainder of the century critics were divided as to opinion on Webster, some (as Moore suggests) praising the 'poetic power of his tragic vision', others unhappy with his 'episodic structure, absurd improbabilities and gross excesses'. Adverse comment of his 'decadence and immorality' is typified in an opinion of Charles Kingsley, 'The strength of Webster's confest mastership lies simply in his acquaintance with vicious nature in general ... [who] handles these horrors with little or no moral purpose'. Once again, a production (this time Horne's at Sadlers Wells in 1850) is marred by cuts, a Victorian softening which blunts Webster's edge. The Athenaeum reporter Lewis asserts that 'we have here not even Webster'. Another critic comments that the production 'lacks that fine humanity which looks so beautiful in Shakespeare'.

Webster's original text only began to be restored unadulterated to an audience in 1892 with William Poel's production which ran up against William Archer's comments. 'Ramshackle looseness of structure and barbarous violence of effect, hideous cacophonies, neither verse nor prose, Bedlam-broke-loose ... poor Webster'. In 1899 Sidney Lee added weight to Archer's argument of Webster's 'true artistic sense ... with a persistence that seems unjustifiable in a great artist ... concentrated his chief energies on repulsive themes and characters'. Such opinions are however countered by Swinburne on Webster's 'command of terror', that 'no poet is morally nobler'. As the century closed there were an increasing number of others ready to adopt a Lamb-like enthusiasm.

TWENTIETH-CENTURY CRITICISM – MODERNIST

The kinds of conflict emblematic of the twentieth century attest to the veracity of Webster's assessment of humankind's inhumanity. Lucas was not the only critic to recognise the poet's up-to-date relevance, in sharp contrast with the nineteenth century's preciousness which decried his brutal **imagery**. Moore recounts how a review in *The Times* of a stage production of the play in 1945 appeared by strange but telling accident immediately beneath some recent pictures of Nazi extermination camps. The world had had to become used to confronting situations of horror again, and their perpetrators were modern Ferdinands and Bosolas.

The twentieth century has been more sympathetic to Webster. T.S. Eliot cites him as a 'genius directed toward chaos' and gives him pride of first two stanzas place in a poem 'Whispers of Immortality':

> Webster was much possessed by death
> And saw the skull beneath the skin;
> And breastless creatures underground
> Leaned backward with a lipless grin.

> Daffodil bulbs instead of balls
> Stared from the sockets of his eyes!
> He knew that thought clings round dead limbs
> Tightening its lusts and luxuries.

Another recent commentator fails to put the playwright alongside other Jacobeans altogether, likening his output to the work of Beckett and Brecht. So that Sir William Watson's intended antagonism towards Webster's characters can in fact be accepted as an admission, albeit reluctant, of the playwright's verisimilitude. 'These men had no sober vision of things. Theirs is a world that reels in a "disastrous twilight" of lust and blood ... Webster is felt as a blurring influence ... Virtue in this disordered world is merely wasted, honour bears not issue, nobleness dies unto itself'.

Rupert Brooke in his *John Webster and the Elizabethan Drama* (Sidgwicke and Jackson, 1916) asserts 'Webster was a great writer; and the way in which one uses great writers is two-fold. There is the exhilarating way of reading their writing; and there is the essence of the whole man'. Symonds, however, leavens his praise of *The Duchess*: 'each part is etched with equal effort after luminous effect upon a murky background; and the whole play is a mosaic of these parts. It lacks the breadth which comes from concentration on a master-motive'.

The truth is that for some modern spectators and critics the language is too mannered and too melodramatic and audiences are reduced to laughter rather than tears. It remains hard in our hard-bitten world for a director to stage a production which is both naturalistic and ghoulish; and too easy to allow dark deeds and stinging language to devolve into poetising fantasy. The play producer too easily forgets, and at his or her peril, Pound's aphorism that 'drama is not words, but people moving about on a stage using words'.

Modernism is almost over by 1960 when Peggy Ashcroft plays the Duchess at the Aldwych. A comment of that performance is a good way in to a short review of the post-modernist period, with its various strands of **feminist, historicist** and deconstructive criticism. Ashcroft's performance of 'gentle raillery, tremulous passion, melting womanliness and utter certainty are blended into something of fragile and almost touchable beauty'.

CONTEMPORARY CRITICISM

Not all the critics in this post-modern period are post-modern. In fact J.R. Mulryne (in Brown and Harris, 1960) reverts back to the positively old-fashioned view of the heroine-**protagonist's** culpability; 'When the Duchess chooses to defy her brothers' world her choice inescapably involves an element of deceit or at best evasion'. Mulryne is not being critical of the playwright, however, but of the main character, and students may find such a stance simplistic. In his critique Mulryne later acknowledges Webster's 'mastery of the theatre, his control of tone and atmosphere'.

Leonora Leet Brodwin introduces a geographist perspective in her 1972 critique. She compares the rugged Amalfi coast with a tragic vision, surviving the wild sea to be shipwrecked on an inhospitable shore. Her Duchess does not long for love and romance so much as the safe haven of harmony and simplicity. She wants her to combine the roles of ruler and lover. She is unfortunate to harbour such healthy desires in such a sick society. Nor can she draw much succour from her husband, 'better suited to be an onlooker than an active participant'. Her mistake is in expecting others to measure up to her standards and logic. Paradoxically, Antonio's weakness brings peace to a marriage whose other partner dominates her world. But when that dominance is lost, his presence of passivity is more than she can bear and she sends him from her company with equanimity. She, but not he, can 'die like a Prince'. So the Duchess must emerge from her dream of happy fantasy, face up to a life apart, the curses of her world of contradictions that give her hope, 'Look you, the stars shine still' (IV.1.99). She is caught between the court and nature. She prefers nature but avers 'I am Duchess of Malfi still' (IV.2.139). By throwing off nobility she embraces mortality, 'the very heights of humanity'. That democratic stance is reinforced by her execution speech; there is no difference between a 'neck broken by rough ropes and one cut by diamonds'. What she gives as a result she gives receiving death, that 'all the wealth of Europe' is worth nothing compared with love. Her temporary revival's purpose seems only to express that love. Such is self-sacrifice. Thus is revenge proved meaningless, even when moved by justifiable anger. That in the end is her redeeming gift to Antonio; that he seeks reconciliation with the Duchess's poisonous brothers, not revenge. We are left to ponder the opposing forces of malignant strength and defenceless compassion, and whether it is possible to move from one to another. Sadly, it seems that malevolence stars; but that even within such a world a tragic dignity can exist.

In contrast with Brodwin's dark analysis, Nicholas Brooke's *Horrid Laughter* (Open Books, 1979) offers a perspective on the dimension of the 'evil of preposterous grandeur ... the logic of definition in death, at horrid laughter at death-in-life'. Jacqueline Pearson in *Tragedy and Tragicomedy in the Plays of John Webster* (Manchester University Press, 1980) changes this slant slightly, demonstrating how **tragedy** is related to other kinds of experience, how a mix of **genre**, tragedy with **comedy** enriches, brings relief and freshness to the plot. So attention is drawn to the wooing scene, a comedy with tragic overtones; to the dance of the mad, where death of sanity operates outside the framework of normality. She iterates that jocularity is a constant companion of tragedy, distancing characters from the audience; the sense to the nonsense paradox of how Ferdinand 'laughs like a deadly cannon'.

Catherine Belsey (1980) adopts a **historicist** position. She places the play 'between the emblematic tradition of the medieval stage and the increasing commitment to realism of the post-Restoration theatre'. She asserts that the play's tension at a point between abstraction and realism informs its construction throughout: so that there is life and death, purity and impurity; there are meetings and plots, cynicism and humour. In each pairing of opposites is a refinement of definition. The problem of that tension is best observed when opposites attempt to coalesce; when evil and power fuse, when love encounters betrayal, when emblematic love must exist alongside the reality of a corrupt world.

The intrinsic paradox of post-modernism is its tendency to orthodoxy. John Selzer writes in his essay *Merit and Degree in Webster's 'The Duchess of Malfi'* (English Literary Renaissance, Winter 1981) that the play has become more written about than almost any other non-Shakespearean **Renaissance tragedy**; on the Duchess's guilt, on Bosola and Ferdinand's motives and on the 'anti-climactic' final act. Selzer makes out a case for the Duchess's exoneration by her attempt to establish a meritocracy in place of the traditional aristocracy. He uses the same argument to mitigate Bosola's guilt, reasoning that the servant's discontentment issues from lack of reward. And Selzer reinforces his theme by suggesting that the final act is an outworking of Bosola's realisation that the master/servant relationship is worthless, confirmed by Delio in the last Act's final speech. The wretched brothers 'Leave no more fame behind 'em' (V.5.113) and the Duchess's only surviving son by Antonio, issue of 'Merit and Degree', inherits the earth.

There is a great deal of **irony** in Jonathan Dollimore's **historicist**-leaning doctoral thesis *Radical Tragedy* (1989). He builds on Selzer's opinion of Webster's tendency towards merit and away from class by stressing the Jacobean's place in a line that includes Montaigne, Spinoza, Machiavelli, Galileo, Rousseau, Hume, Kant, Nietzsche, Hegel, Marx, Gramsci, Althusser, Brecht and Foucault; meritocrats all, stressing 'the decentring of man'. It is the refusal to be subservient, the demythologising of state power and religious force, which both threatens its practitioner-ideologues and imbues them with compelling life-energy. Dollimore compares and allies Webster's meritocrats with Brecht's *Mother Courage* (1941).

In recent years, interest in studying Webster's play alongside Lope's has emerged. Cynthia Rodriguez-Badendyck exemplifies this new focus in her *The Duchess of Malfi's Steward* (1985), an examination of the role of Antonio in the drama. Although contemporary with each other (*The Duchess*, 1614, *The Steward*, 1618), it is unlikely that Lope and Webster knew about each other's work. Badendyck shows that both are sympathetic to the Duchess in the teeth of the then current trend of their sources to show negativity towards her. Badendyck cautions against the assumption of adopting too revolutionary a flavour for the plays although, she asserts, there is no 'denying that the luminous figure of the Duchess is perfectly capable of dominance'. She goes on to claim that it is strong women's very strength which 'functions to support their sagging superiors', by implication weak men, thus shoring up rather than imperilling the status quo, never threatening male power. We are in a diseased world, 'out of joint ... [where] everyman is a woman'; where men are under, impotent (except in sexual mechanics). The dilemma this presents is met in Lope's same-source text by masculinising Antonio (who becomes energetic and effective) and by Webster in demonising Bosola (who becomes scheming and ruthless). Webster's Antonio is passive and immaturely ambivalent about sexuality; he wants his virtuous Duchess passive not passionate. Lope's Antonio is full of intense sensuality, 'knowing' about desire and wanting his Duchess vital and lubricious. Thus Webster's play devolves into a nightmarish quality of fantasy and loss of identity. Lope's concentrates, however, not on isolation and despair but on reality and integrity. The divergence in the two plays' ethos is in large measure due to a divergence in focus; Webster's on how things fall apart, Lope's on how things come together.

A review of contemporary criticism needs to incorporate some comment on James MacTaggart's BBC production (1972). The performance was the subject of qualified acclaim by Raymond Williams in *The Independent* in July 1987. He reported on the frequent mid-twentieth-century tendency to show the action of the play as farce, a throw-back to Eliot's 'Sweeney Agonistes' and a throw-forward to the mid '60s 'Theatre of the Absurd'. He dismisses the implication of Ferdinand's incest as Freudian obsession and compliments the play's sober recognition of anger, confusion and violence, the ridicule or ritual 'murderously destructive of isolated appetites'. Perfect marriage, says Antonio, is not domesticity but economics, husbandry.

Finally we will look briefly at a study undertaken in 1998 of comparisons between Lope and Webster's plays. Eva Cruz Garcia is critical of Badendyck's acceptance of the primary role in the story of romantic love, suggesting that such is a cultural myth. She sets the often articulated problem of the Duchess's innocence or guilt against the steward's ambition being mitigated by his love, 'Antonio's morals or propriety are hardly ever questioned'. What Eva Cruz questions is the central importance of the Duchess's widowhood. What she stresses is the role that the service of an intimate counsellor plays; and whether 'female involvement with servants is corruption' epitomised by the Duchess's manifest lack of those Puritan qualities essential to a marriage within ordered society, patient suffering, mildness, humility, chastity, loyalty and obedience – 'qualities needed in a servant', Ms Cruz claims. The thrust of her thesis is 'how effortlessly the language of service becomes the language of love'.

We may reflect on how the Duchess's demands of Antonio to treat her 'like a man' become submerged in Webster's play into an implicit plea by Antonio for her to treat him like a woman, his ultimate acknowledgement that her superior status of class more than outweighs his superior status as a man.

In one respect post-modern/deconstructionist criticism radically departs from all the criticisms that have gone before – and that is that it is fundamentally parasitical. Rather than developing a new insight, it takes sociological insights of its own era, for instance **Feminism**, and applies these to pre post-modernist texts. Feminist critics will therefore look for aspects of a **Renaissance** play which seem to lend themselves to a feminist interpretation.

This is not a critique of post-modern criticism, itself essentially ill-defined and with strongly anarchic tendencies. If anything, it is a commendation of a **genre** of such robust independence, where logic is in symbiosis with experiment. Students will wish to investigate how this kind of thinking can be applied in greater detail to *The Duchess of Malfi*.

BIBLIOGRAPHY

THE TEXT

Elizabeth M. Brennan, ed., *The Duchess of Malfi*, New Mermaids, A & C Black, 1993

> This is the edition of the text used in the preparation of this Note. It includes full
> comments on the text itself, helpful notes on the editions of the play and a detailed
> discussion of a number of topics in the introduction

John Russell Brown, ed., *The Duchess of Malfi*, The Revels Plays, Manchester University Press, 1964

> The Revels edition includes comprehensive notes and appendices and a fine introduction to the play

F.L. Lucas, ed., *The Complete Works of John Webster*, Chatto & Windus, 1927

> In four volumes, this is still the definitive edition of the text extant. Of special interest is the General Introduction in Volume I and the Commentary and Textual Notes in Volume II

GENERAL REFERENCES

R.W. Dent, *John Webster's Borrowing*, University of California Press, 1960

> An encyclopedic piece of thorough research listing line by line Webster's use of other authors' previous material. Of particular interest is the Chapter devoted to 'The Duchess of Malfi', itself ninety pages long

Cynthia Rodriguez-Badendyck, *The Duchess of Malfi's Steward*, Doverhouse, 1985

> Published in Canada, an English translation of Lope de Vega's Spanish drama, with a useful introduction comparing Lope's play with Webster's

CRITICISM

Leonora Leet Brodwin, *Elizabethan Love Tragedy 1587–1625*, University of London Press, 1972

> The author examines the relationship of Compassion to Worldly Love, particularly in a chapter entitled 'The Compassionate Vision of The Duchess of Malfi'

Jonathan Dollimore, *Radical Tragedy*, Harvester Wheatsheaf, 1989

> Particularly the chapters on 'Contexts', 'Subjectivity and Social Process' and 'Transgression Without Virtue', this book takes an **historicist** stance and is quoted in this Note in the section on Critical History

ARTICLES & PAPERS

Catherine Belsey, *Emblem and Antithesis in 'The Duchess of Malfi'*, Renaissance Drama, 1980
> This essay explores Webster's position between the medieval tradition of 'moral types' and the realist theatre of psychological analysis

Eva Cruz Garcia, *Love and Service in Lope de Vega's 'El mayordomo de la Duquesa de Amalfi' and John Webster's 'Duchess of Malfi'*, 1998 [Unpublished Dissertation]
> Especially valuable in drawing out significant comparisons between the two plays and in a section on 'Counsel' as a theme

OTHER READING

The more enquiring student may wish to enquire further, and the following will be helpful for a more in-depth understanding:

Lisa Jardine, *Still Harping on Daughters: Women and Drama in the Age of Shakespeare*, Harvester Wheatsheaf, 1989
> For a balanced presentation of a radical **feminist** viewpoint

John Russell Brown and Bernard Harris, eds, *Jacobean Theatre*, Edward Arnold, 1960
> An anthology and of particular interest is Chapter IX written by J.R. Mulryne, 'The White Devil and The Duchess of Malfi'

Note: Students are recommended to read Webster's other major play, *The White Devil*.

VIDEO

Best attend a live performance. Video material is not widely available, but some libraries have copies of the play, presented by the BBC in 1972 (Directed by James MacTaggart). Seeing as well as hearing the play will add greatly to the enjoyment and understanding that reading it gives.

Recommended is reference to a workmanlike dictionary of literary terms, a good example of which is Martin Gray, *A Dictionary of Literary Terms* (York Handbooks, York Press/Longman, 1992). Meanwhile, collected here is an abbreviation of a few of the more useful terms relevant to this Note.

alliteration relating to the texture or onomatopoeic nature of language; words which start with similar sounding consonants coming close together in the text (also sometimes known as head-rhyme)

Aristotelian drama Aristotle was a Greek philosopher of the fourth century BC who endeavoured to deduce what were the essential ingredients for theatrical success. Later defined as the Unities, his studies incorporated plot, theme, narrative technique, characterisation and the handling of time and place

aside a device in common use in drama whereby a character addresses the audience whilst other characters are still on stage. (It contrasts with soliloquy when a character on stage alone addresses the audience.) It is normally the playwright's intention that what is said is said sincerely

Augustan originally a golden age of Roman literature a hundred years before and after the time of the birth of Christ when the writing of Horace, Virgil and Ovid flourished. The term is now usually applied to a period of English writing in the first half of the eighteenth century, notably of Addison, Steele, Pope and Swift. The style common to both periods is one of taste, refinement and patriotism

blank verse a form of dramatic writing adopted almost universally in the Elizabethan and Jacobean periods, and normally consisting of iambic pentameters. Webster employs it throughout the play, except in the case of a rare use of prose

characterisation the technique by which a writer clothes the personae of his story (play, novel, etc) to make them credible

closure how authors achieve a feeling of finality in their work. Closure is a given requirement of Renaissance drama, whether in comedy or tragedy. Modern writers and critics have abandoned this figure to leave texts and their interpretations open to the reader's questioning

comedy a drama which ends in happiness for its characters after a period of trouble. Comedy has its origins in the Greece of the fifth century BC

dénouement how the plot of a narrative (of whatever genre) finally resolves itself

double entendre an ambiguous remark; often a pun with sexual connotations

dramatic irony a commonly used dramatic device which places the audience in possession of information the characters do not have

feminism a philosophy embracing economics, politics, literature and indeed every aspect of the humanities, and which seeks to posit women on an equal footing with men; and in doing so to show how men have established and reinforced their historical dominance. The development of feminism has been rapid since 1945 but was articulated much earlier by Mary Wollstonecraft and Virginia Woolf

genre a category of text, e.g. poetry, drama, biography, fiction etc. *The Duchess of Malfi* is Drama, more specifically Tragedy (sub-genre). We are entitled to be more specific still and refer to it as Revenge Tragedy (sub-sub-genre)

historicism the practice of placing ideas within an historical context, much in vogue by those literary critics who look for textual links with events within a cultural framework

humanism a system of thought, particularly applicable to literature, emanating from Classical origins, having its apotheosis in the Europe of the Renaissance. Humanism's philosophical essence is the reason and dignity of mankind

iambic pentameter an iamb is the term used for the most common metrical foot in English poetry, short stress followed by long, ti-tum. Five iambs in one line together comprise in turn the commonest pattern in English verse. Webster only departs from the verse of iambic pentameter when he strays, rarely, into prose. The last couplet of the play, duly scanned, looks like this:

Integrity of life is fame's best friend,
Which nobly, beyond death, shall crown the end

imagery language which builds up a picture or image (e.g. by the use of metaphor or simile)

innuendo a phrase or remark which can have a double meaning, one of which is usually uncomplimentary and possibly sexually suggestive. Innuendo compares with pun and double entendre

irony when what is said/written is in contention or contrast with what is meant

malcontent a person common in Jacobean society as well as drama, the role carries connotations of melancholia and dissatisfaction, often quite reasonably so, and is often directed against the excesses of court life

metaphor something described as being something else and 'carrying over' these associations (see simile)

oleaginous verbally ingratiating, 'oily'

onomatopoeia words which sound like the noise they describe

oxymoron a kind of paradox when two contradictory terms are juxtaposed improbably e.g. 'This is terrible good counsel' (I.2.232)

parody an imitation of a work of prose or poetry construed in such a way as to ridicule; ways to effect this are often by exaggeration or mock solemnity

persona/personae person or persons who have imposed on them points of view expressed in the written work which are not necessarily those of the author. In novels, the persona might be a first person narrator; in drama each character fulfils that role when the speaking is with them

prose 'straightforward' writing without recourse to the patterned regularity of metred verse. It can encompass speech or description or narrative. (Prose poetry has the ornateness and imagery of poetry but, like prose, has no discernible metre.) Bosola is the character for whom Webster most consistently employs prose

protagonist usually the leading character/hero in a piece of writing, and here the Duchess. A looser definition may suggest that more than one character can be part of a body of protagonists

pun one word with more than one meaning, often very different and used in ways to set up a witty joke or comic play, in good or poor taste. Compares with innuendo, metaphor and double entendre

Renaissance coined in the nineteenth century looking back at that period of European history, following the Middle Ages, when knowledge of all kinds took a great leap forward and was subject to a 'rebirth'. Elizabethan and Jacobean drama come broadly at the peak of this brilliantly creative period. Parallel in English literature and science with this humanist movement was the religious Reformation

rhetoric writing and speaking intended to persuade. In modern parlance, rhetoric is used derogatorily. Criticism is a modern form of rhetoric

satire a humorous and usually ironic aggression on human or institutional imperfection or folly, characterised by a ridiculing mockery of the morally degenerate, doubtful or absurd, by a witty comparison with the ideal, or at least the preferred

Senecan tragedy incorporates the Revenge Tragedy at which Webster excelled. The Roman poet Seneca adapted Greek drama for non-theatrical presentation, formalising certain essential characteristics – declamation, dialogue, revenge, disaster, the ghost and the nurse; all in five Acts

simile when one thing is said to be 'like' another, always containing the words 'like' or 'as', and inviting a comparison

soliloquy the speech to an audience by a character alone on the stage. The convention is that this 'speaking aloud' is a reliable reflection of the persona's true inner thoughts and feelings. In this way the audience is given information in a form of dramatic irony not revealed to the other characters in the play. Critics cite Bosola as a master of the craft. Perhaps craft is an apposite word. We should beware the reliability of what is said in apparent intimate confidence to the audience in soliloquy when the actor is aware of not being alone. See aside

solipsism a self-centred view of the world which holds that nothing of relevance exists outside oneself

sophism an argument intended to mislead

tone how language is used to engender a prevailing mood of behaviour. Tone can be as much 'heard' by a reader of the written word as by the spectator in a theatre and is imparted by syntax and vocabulary. It can be undermined by devices such as irony, so that what is said is not what the speaker intends to be heard

tragedy has a wide literary application (drama and novel) in which is portrayed the career and downfall of the protagonist (often an heroic figure)

trope language which is figurative, decorative and rhetorical rather than literal, used in word or phrase, e.g. images such as metaphor and simile